DAY OF THUNDER YEARS OF WOE!

Mr. President, Mr. President,

Mr. President

This book is dedicated to my grandchildren and great grandchildren. Each of you is dynamic and can achieve your dreams.

You are blessed to have outstanding parents. We, your parents your grandparents and I, are proud of you. We love you and seek the best for you.

Grandchildren

Sarah, Lea, Ashley, Anthony, Jr., .Amber, Devin, Justin, Tannera, Taylor, David, Jr., Colby, Jordan, Chardae, Jalen, Ryan, Gregory, Jr., Kahlil, Isaac, Amarie, Paytn, Zoie and Zachary

Great Grandchildren

Derion and Demi

Mr. President, Mr. President, Mr. President

Copyrighted © *2011 by Tanner M. George, Sr.*
Author

Printed in the United States of America by

APM Publishing Company

admin@apmpublishingco.com

Contents

Mr. President

1943

Spring on the Potomac

Chapter 1

6

Mr. President, it is the spring of 1943. *The republicans and some democrats are screaming that your spending is sending the deficit so over the top, our children and grandchildren will never recover. They say that your new deal programs are nothing but the scourge of capitalism. Senator Melvyn and some of his republican cronies are actually accusing you of pushing socialism. They are actually calling you a socialist sir.*

Sitting across from the President and flanked by the President's cabinet, Mark Linden, President Frank Dean Robertson's Chief of Staff, continued, *although they support your war spending Mr. President, they claim that you are going way overboard with your call for a tax increase. Just this morning, Congressman Samuel Nelson, you know, the minority whip, said you were destroying the country's future with your social programs. Mr. President,* chimed in Vice President Dan Blake, *the country is involved in a war not of its making.*

The few factories that are operating are roaring at full capacity. We need many more factories turning out the products needed by our troops. We must support the troops and prosecute the war. I strongly encourage your efforts to do what the constitution demands, which is to protect and defend as well as to serve the common good. I say full speed ahead, Mr. President. The American people will back you because they know your policies are right for the country. Full speed ahead, I say.

Damn the republicans and their stay put attitude. We need action, your kind of action, and we need it now, fumed Vice President Dan Blake. Nods of approval from the assembled cabinet assured Robertson that he had the full support of his key administrators.

The basic cabinet rule was to sit through these meetings. Rising slowly from his chair at the presidential conference table, President Robertson violated this rule by choosing to stand. A Polio victim, Frank Dean Robertson seldom stood. When he did, he used two canes for stability.

I wish to share with you in confidence something that every President has known and shared with his top advisors since the inception of the union. The strength and security of the nation is heavily dependent on all of the people sharing in the benefits of this great country.

History shows dictators and their favored groups being violently thrown aside by their constituents who have grown weary of being denied, while those who govern them and their pals live lavishly, the President volunteered. Continuing with his speech, Robertson said, w*e are all capitalists and favor a strong capitalist society.*

Good capitalism is when wealth comes up from the bottom through investments, hard work and loans. Each of us is rich; and we made our fortunes through good capitalism. Warming to his task, Robertson noted, *there is no socialism in our blood or policies. Nevertheless, all Americans and even illegal immigrants must share in the riches of this great country.*

This must include poor whites, Negros, Puerto Ricans and Mexicans. His voice rising, the President went on, *we rich people, from industrialists to bankers, stand squarely on the shoulders of the poorest Americans. Even though they make damning public statements about government spending on social programs, the loudest legislative protestor of these programs will find some way to vote for compromise versions that don't sound like give a-ways.*

Every President and leaders of congress know that public funds should mostly go to improve the common good, and for defense. This does not include lining the pockets of fat cats with taxpayer dollars. The adage that is etched in American stone is "riches come from capitalism." Capitalism starts with people who have the least to spend. Taxpayer dollars create jobs and provide the means that help common folks survive and rise. **Taxpayer money must never go to enrich the fortunes of millionaires.**

Let it never be forgotten, Robertson advised, *common Americans send their sons to die so that our rich asses can stay home in safety. Poor people toil for minimum subsistence wages so we can enjoy the good life on their sweaty backs. It's their resources that pay for teachers, policemen and firemen to protect our bodies and our property, as well as to educate our children.*

Heed my word, If we get to a place of wide separation of wealth between the haves and the have-nots, trouble will swiftly follow for us haves. If the middle class and the poor become disillusioned by a wide disparity of wealth between rich Americans and average Americans, we could find ourselves coming to the same end as every dictator and his rich henchmen; that is, uprising by the populace. So, make no mistake. No matter the vitriol with which the opposition and their press attack, taxpayer money will only be used for a strong defense and to provide for the "common good."

Which means that we are obligated to create and maintain programs that elevate the everyday American. By doing so, we will uplift the country. We will keep the nation safe and strong, with a dedicated populace. Feeling invigorated, President Robertson explained, *therein underlies the premise of providing public assistance to the general populace, including the middle class and poor.*

Some of the money that the government prints will go to banks. The banks lend to small businesses to create jobs. Through public schools, some funds will help our youth obtain an education. Other money will be used to assist our returning warriors. Part of the funds will help to build highways, runways, bridges, railroads and other infrastructure for our people to travel from place to place. And yes, there will be money for the unemployed and others who are down on their luck. These funds include food allowances, medical care and shelter assistance for those who cannot afford these necessities.

*Irrespective of citizenship, an equal amount of money is printed for every person who can provide an address; and is counted by the census. The poor receive about twenty five cents of every dollar that is printed in their names. The funds that the poor receive are immediately spent with hundreds of thousands of eagerly awaiting merchants. Together with retirees and military personnel, the poor form **America's economic base**. These are also people from whom the economy extracts cheap labor.*

Let me digress, said the President. *As I alluded to before, taxpayer money must not be given directly to rich people for any reason. Republicans say that the rich will create jobs from government money. They say that if the government will give them money through tax breaks, the rich will invest those funds in businesses that produce jobs. The truth is, it just doesn't happen that way. Most of that free money will languish in their pockets, while the remainder will find its way into expensive homes, lavish outings, fancy cars, yachts, ladies of the night and rare paintings, but not in jobs.*

13

Mr. President

1993

Summer on the Potomac

Chapter 2

Investing and borrowing are the means by which businesses are financed. Raising capital through public stock sales is the way that corporations fund themselves. People tend to protect and increase their investments. Creditors lean on borrowers to perform and repay their loans. There is no personal incentive for individuals who receive corporate and rich man welfare to invest those funds in job creating businesses. Money given to rich people will be spent only in a few places. It will not circulate in the economy. The economy needs circulation, not money expulsion, finished Robertson.

***Mr. President, it is the summer of 1993.** We are about to balance the budget. Admittedly we are doing so with the help of a large tax increase. This will allow us to put millions to work,* spoke treasury secretary Levi Hamilton. *With unemployment up, the economy in a shambles, and inflation on the rise, you would think that some of those elephants would display modicums of statesmanship and help,* Hamilton continued.

15

. *The mid-term elections are less than a year away. We must move with dispatch to get your agenda put in place,* ended Hamilton. President Walter James Collins, a senator from a small state, had come from nowhere to win the presidency a year earlier. Exuding a character filled with charisma and charm, the President seemed more a swashbuckling romantic instead of a hardened politician. He had come under vicious attack for alleged sexual indiscretions.

The attacks continued and expanded into Collin's presidency in the form of criminal investigations of his and his wife's real estate deals. Although it appeared that the accusations were trumped up, the republicans demanded that the President appoint a special prosecutor to investigate the charges. Finally, Collins yielded to republican demands and named a special prosecutor to look into the allegations. Urged on by republicans, the Special prosecutor pursued the President with unrelenting vigor.

The President was heavily dependent on his wife, Helen Collins. The first lady radiated beauty and grace that would befit the most admired Hollywood starlet. Her stunning appearance belied the fact that she was a shrewd and skillful politician in her own right. Rumor had it that President Collins sought her advice on everything affecting his presidency.

I fully agree with Secretary Hamilton, exclaimed Vice President Arthur Gaines. *Your briefing to this cabinet earlier was most timely, Mr. President. The American people are hurting and we must move with dispatch to begin the healing process. The trickle-down theory of past administrations is a bunch of crock. The only thing that has trickled is the American people's money pouring into the coffers of very rich people.* VP Gaines ended with; *we need to get this tax bill passed before the mid-terms. History shows that the party in power always loses one or both houses of congress in the mid-term elections.*

President Collins, it is the year 1999, exclaimed Senate Majority Leader Robert Levine. *Three cheers to you and your team on what will go down in history as one of the most successful administrations ever. You inherited a devastated economy and turned it around. You presided over the beginning of a global economy. In spite of the republicans tracking you in what appeared to be a perverted effort to fondle your genitals, you balanced the budget, reformed welfare and won a war without a single casualty.*

If that is not a record of which any President could be proud, we project that you will leave the country with a sizable surplus when you exit office, exclaimed Levine, now fully into his dialogue. Orating further, he continued, *at this very moment Mr. President, I am so proud to be an American.* Stroking his beard, Levine added, *I feel good about the condition of our country. Yet, I can't shake this nagging feeling that something very subtle and sinister appears to be in the offing for our nation.*

I am greatly disturbed at our hi-tech companies for moving most of our hi-tech jobs to foreign countries. Sure we have full employment, but the recent jobs are mostly service oriented. During the past two republican administrations, rich cats got richer. We lost mainstay industries such as steel; and union busting caused a decline in labor unions. What I am saying here Mr. President is that you have done a great job in running the country. Yet, I am afraid that the trend started by the previous two republican administrations will continue and do serious damage to our great country.

I thank you sir for listening to me today. I also thank the cabinet and you congressional leaders for your attentiveness, Levine, nodding in the direction of the cabinet and congressional leaders who were part of the president's audience, said as he sat down. President Collins responded, *Mr. Majority Leader, I thank you for that most incisive and highly enlightening information. Permit me to share something with you that every President comes to know.*

19

Our country's successful continuation depends on all of the people sharing in the benefits that this nation has to offer. The people see those who govern them living lavishly, while they, the common folks, suffer in poverty. Dictators and their cohorts usually wind up with their heads rolling down the street; defending themselves in a Nuremburg court or being forced into exile by their constituents who grow weary of the disparity in wealth between them and their so called leaders.

The republicans viciously lie when they say that we are trying to promote socialism, railed Collins. *You don't have to be a socialist to know that all Americans and even illegal immigrants must share in this country's wealth, including poor Whites, Negroes, Puerto Ricans and Latinos. The best kept financial secret is:* **"rich people can't be rich, without the poor."** *Jobs and a sound economy are not created by the rich. The poor create jobs and stabilize an economy by spending their small sums in myriads of retail places. This prolific and diverse spending make for a viable economy.*

Rich people, who bother to think, know that their fountain of plenty flows from poor and middle income people. Wealthy people stand squarely on the shoulders of the poorest Americans. It would be pure folly if the weight of rich people' wealth broke the financial backs of those who support them. You hear these "poor excuses for politicians" out there running their campaigns against welfare cheats and deadbeats.

Those are just catch phrases aimed at the racist tendencies of the politicians' White constituents. They portray Black Americans as lazy and shiftless vagabonds who take food from hard working White people. This is nothing new. It's the way these ragged politicians have used racism for decades to try to win elections, President Collins said as he launched into one of his pet peeves.

These politicians know nothing about the issues. It's just to the everlasting credit of White people that most of them are beginning to see these stinkpots for what they are; a sniveling bunch who have to rely on racism to get elected.

These idiots use nasty racial smoke screens to cover their ignorance and to fool White people into voting for them. Well, their odious strategies are coming back to haunt them because White voters have begun to reject those ruthless tactics. Also, the new welfare reform bill, which I signed into law, renders void that evil strategy. This is much to the republicans chagrin and election losses. I am going to wrap this up, said the President, *by saying that corporate welfare costs the country much more than the meager stipends that poor people receive.*

Practically every dollar earned by some high paid worker is tinged with government money. Bailouts, pork barrel spending that makes rich congressional constituents richer, defense and other government contracts for useless equipment and worthless projects are just some examples of corporate welfare. A fired up President Walter J. Collins lashed out. *So when you hear a fat cat berating those who receive government help or a politician orating against welfare cheats and dead beats, ask about the source of their income.*

Those who claim that they work hard, but others are shiftless and don't want to work, should ask themselves; am I providing my own income or am I dependent on someone else for my job. Ask them to trace the origin of their financial good fortune. Odds are some government money is in their financial good fortune. Speaking forcefully, President Collins reiterated his position on taxpayer funds. Every President and leaders of congress know that public funds should mostly be spent to serve the common good. I applaud any and all Americans who earn their wealth through good old fashioned capitalism. I'll fight to the death for the right of anyone to honestly convert their skills, investments, loans and sweat into as much wealth as possible.

As for the global economy; it can be a very good thing for the country, or it can be a very bad thing for the country. The global economy can and will make many people very rich. It will also leave some rich people penniless. I certainly share Leader Levine's concerns about American jobs being shipped overseas.

Mr. President

2003

Fall on the Potomac

Chapter 3

Our next President must protect our country against multi-national corporations. Lining the pockets of corporate executives with taxpayer dollars serves the good of the wealthy, not the common good. Taxpayers' funds are meant to create jobs, defend the country, insure sound national infrastructure and help common folks. Taxpayer dollars must never be used to increase the affluence of millionaires and multi-millionaires, Having finished his meeting, President Collins retired to his private quarters.

Mr. President, it is the year 2003*. Oops, I meant to say Mr. Vice President,* laughingly intoned Defense Secretary John Sanger. *As much as I hate the terrorist action that was visited on defenseless citizens, it opened up some wonderful opportunities for us. Before the plane attack, the President's numbers were less than dismal. Now, his favorable poll numbers are as high as they can get. The country feels good about the President and is poised to give him anything that he wants. This type of enthusiasm is rare for any President.*

Let's not squander this wave of goodwill that the President is receiving, continued the Secretary. *Yes we declared war against the terrorists and the government that harbored them. After we defeated them, we installed a new government that we can control. I'll admit that was excitingly successful. Look,* said Sanger, *our military rolled in and kicked some Arab ass, but it was not tested in that operation. Ok, we displayed our air might in the Gulf War.* Showing some frustration, Sanger admitted, *we didn't test our ground weapons, our boots on the ground forces or the many naval and air resources that we have at our command.*

We need new targets on which to practice. Hell, we have some new shock bombs that sound like nuclear explosions when they hit. In reality though, they are actually conventional weapons. We need to see the reactions of targeted enemy officials to those bomb explosions, pleaded Sanger. *I betcha they will be in a mood to surrender, or at least talk favorably. Seeing their reactions would be worth the bomb drops alone,* concluded Sanger.

Mr. Vice President, interjected Secretary of the Treasury Miller Payne. *I agree with the Secretary of Defense about testing our weapons in a more comprehensive war. In the meantime, we can take advantage of the large surplus that Collins was kind enough to leave us. We should put that money into the pockets of the President's and your base; you know, the very wealthy, of which we are a part. That money does not belong in the country's treasury. Senators and congressmen are pissing all over themselves to get their hands on that money, supposedly for their constituencies.*

We also need to reward the rich, the ultra rich and the corporations that support us with some of that tax money. Miller Payne continued. *Look Mr. Vice President, now that we have a republican controlled House, a republican controlled Senate and a republican in the White House, there are so many things that we can do. Corporations that are relocating many of their operations to foreign countries are lobbying for taxpayer assistance to pay for those large moves.*

I strongly support your position to give them these tax breaks. I confess, however, that I don't see how these relocations will benefit American workers, particularly those displaced by the moves. Yet I accept the corporations' premise that the process will free up capital. They insist that they will invest that freed up capital in American businesses. On a roll, Payne volunteered, *many regulations imposed on big business by the recently demised democratic administration are actually hardships on some of these companies. We should take the chains of these businesses and let them run.*

There's no telling what they can do for the economy if we gave them more latitude. This must include relaxing environmental restrictions. Heck, I have been informed by reputable scientists that this green house crap is a bunch of bull. We should just ignore those so called environmental scientists Mr. Vice President, urged Miller Payne, taking his seat. *Thanks Miller. You have expressed my sentiments exactly,* replied Vice President Martin Dobbs.

Rising from his desk chair, Vice President Martin Dobbs moved around to the front of his desk. *I asked you three trusted friends to meet with me and give me your honest assessments of what the country needs. Each of you is in a crucial position, and we need your input. Give us your report from the Treasurer's perspective Bob,* the vice president asked Robert Tucker, the United States' Treasurer. *Well Mr. Vice President, I'm in complete agreement with everything that's been said.*

Our only problem is that the tax cut and war will deplete our surplus and the country will incur a large deficit. Don't get me wrong; running a deficit is not a bad thing. I'm sure you already know that some of our friends in the auto and airline industries are looking to us to bail them out of their financial malaises, added Tucker. *What we give them will also add to the deficit. That too will not present a problem. How can we free up funds for these and other pressing needs? Not to worry, all of our financial needs can be met by borrowing from foreign sources, notably China.*

That attack on our country has given us big stick opportunity to do unprecedented things. We can now make the world over in our own image, Mr. Vice President. We must be mindful to give the working people some financial award from our tax cut, effused Tucker. *How does six hundred dollars sound for everyone who files an income tax return,* interrupted Treasury Secretary Miller Payne. *That sounds about right Miller,* agreed Treasurer Robert Tucker. *It will be a beautiful sight. Picture this.*

We will create the equivalence of sending a hundred semi trailer trucks to empty the Federal Reserve banks. As we make our get-away through the streets, we toss greenbacks from one of the trucks to the peasants. Adding music and fanfare will give a festive air to the occasion. The people will all be happy to receive their six hundred dollars, including the police, who will scamper to get their share. It's the type of thing from which romance cometh, beamed Treasurer Tucker, now feeling poetic.

Ironically, those over paid news hounds and cable talk show clowns will get enough refunds to make even the most liberal ones sing our praises to the country. This world is getting so over populated that we must have a survival strategy in place. First we form a super elite society that maintains information about everything and everybody. Following up on Payne's "more targets" espousal, Treasurer Tucker noted, yes *we need to control oil rich middle east countries.* **But our main targets must be the citizens and the treasury of the United States of America.**

We do not need a strong middle class. We must create a class of controlling multi-millionaires and billionaires that are as far removed from the general public as the Greek gods were from the average person. We need the poor, the near poor and the controlling wealthy elite, of which we are part. We need government money flowing directly into our vaults. China, India and other low wage countries can manufacture most everything we use at a fraction of the cost to do the same job here.

Nearing the end of his diatribe, Secretary Tucker continued to spout; *small businesses need to be mostly service oriented. The near poor can manage these service businesses that employ the poor, ala the McDonalds of the world. You will see more and more Chinese, African and Indian mid level managers in American businesses. This is good for us. Let China, India, African countries and other nations run our businesses. This way, we can cut back what we spend on education.*

Continuing where Tucker left off, Vice President Dobbs entered the conversation with, *not only does this leave more tax money for us; cut backs in funding for education will reduce the sizable leftist intelligentsia that infects the country. We must increase the strength of our already strong criminal justice system that is serviced by our privately owned prisons. The private criminal institutions can use larger numbers of indentured convict labor to manufacture more products that can supplement the cheap goods which we get from our overseas manufacturing plants.*

By keeping jobs out of the Cities, and making sure that drugs and guns are plentiful, we are assured of a steady supply of manpower to produce goods for our prison network, added Dobbs. *We already know that the Judges and prosecutors could not get on with law firms because they are mostly C and D students.*

Hell, they need the steady paychecks that come from the government. In the Cities, judges, prosecutors, prison officials and even policemen are highly motivated to see that Blacks and Hispanics are continually run through the prison door.

In just one City I personally witnessed these predominantly White, heartless asses plea bargain hundreds of those ignorant street bastards in a week. Let me stop, intoned Dobbs. *When I get wound up, I could go on all day. Our day of plenty and redemption has arrived on the wings of some airplanes, as unfortunate as that was. We must and will seize this historic moment, I'm glad we had the opportunity to talk. It will help me prepare for Burns,* ended the Vice President.

Mr. President, *your approval numbers are off the chain,* offered an elated Vice President Dobbs as he shook hands with President Gray Burns. *Let me extend my Congratulations to you! You have just declared mission accomplished and taken control of that oil rich country in the Middle East. You are also conducting winning wars on two fronts, which means that you actually own those two productive countries. You can now declare yourself the successful War President. This is huge for our finances and for the tax reduction bill that we pushed through congress. Our base, the rich, is quite happy with this tax decrease because it mostly benefits them,* said an elated Martin Dobbs.

Do you remember the natural gas pipe line that we wanted to run out the mountains of Tora Bora to the sea, but kept getting sidetracked by that stupid government? Well it is now a done deal. We have replaced the old government with our government. Not only that, we have successfully installed our government in that oil rich nation. In fact we have already appointed our own Governor there.

Who says that colonialism doesn't work. It just takes the right colonialists to pull it off. That Mr. President is us, said an obviously enthused Vice President Dobbs, as he and President Burns chatted in a private anteroom off the oval office. Burns used this room for very private meetings. *The military industrial complex is so happy, they are filling our pockets with more money than we can ever use. Sanger and those Pentagon yahoos are constantly jerking off because they are having heaps of fun playing with their new military toys. All is good here on the home front as well. The economy is doing great with jobs leading the way.*

Our hi-tech corporate buddies are moving their companies to India, China and other poor ass countries with all due haste. Taking credit, Dobbs voiced, *this was started when we dumped more than a trillion dollars of taxpayer money in their laps. Hell, some of the corporate execs were so excited they could not stop crapping for a week. Did you know Gray that our tax reduction produced a new crop of multi-millionaire corporate CEO's?*

We also made some billionaires out of multimillionaires with our tax cut, declared Dobbs. *Since we deregulated the banking industry, the banks are falling all over themselves making money. Let me tell you what these slick fools are doing in real estate,* offered Dobbs. *Say that a credit risk buyer gets a house at one thousand dollars per month house note. Now that house note is based on maybe a four percent variable interest rate.*

In the fine print is a provision that will send that interest rate as high as twelve and maybe fifteen percent in five years. That part of the interest rate is not discussed with the buyer, Dobbs added while scratching his chin. *If the variable interest rate is questioned by the borrower/buyer, the buyer is usually told that he has five years to raise his salary to cover the increase in house payments. The buyer is very anxious to close the loan because he is getting a big beautiful house with low mortgage payments. Because he knows that his poor credit gets him rejected for credit cards, furniture, car and other time purchases, he is fearful that he may also be disqualified for the house loan. As a result, the buyer leaps to consummate the house purchase. He basically disregards the fact that his initial one thousand dollar monthly mortgage payments will more than double in five years.*

Mr. President. Listen to how the banks make their money. You won't believe this. Little banks make the loans to home buyers, and immediately sell those loans to the big banks for say two points (two percent) or three thousand dollars on a $150,000 loan. The big banks buy up and bundle a number of these loans to sell to traders or end users.

Vice President Dobbs, savoring this time where he has the President's ear and can impress him with his wide ranging knowledge; spoke on, *directly or through traders the big banks say to pension funds or other end users, "you buy this bundle now for two year's interest at the final rate of twelve percent and you will get twenty five years or thirty five years (whether a thirty year or forty year mortgage) at twelve percent interest with no effort on your part."*

That's not bad for guaranteed interest. Well twelve percent on a $150,000 loan is $18,000, which is what the pension fund expects to earn each year from that mortgage. If a bank buys one of these loans for two percent, and sells it for two years' interest at twelve percent, that big bank will receive $36,000 per loan. When $3,000, the cost to the big bank of acquiring the loan from a small bank, is subtracted, the big bank nets $33,000 per loan. Since a big bank's bundles usually contain more than a hundred thousand loans, that bank will make over three billion dollars, and it will not have produced anything, explained Martin Dobbs.

Think of how many billions the banks will make from packaging five to ten million loans just like that every year. That's the range of the number of home loans done each year, phrased Dobbs. *Our personal investments are also doing well. Aside from our publicly known business involvements, our unknown company has holdings in everything from oil to commodities, to banking, insurance and cars,* Dobbs proudly announced to President Burns.

Hell, we even own stock in airline companies and defense industry companies. If anything involving major finances moves, we make money from it, declared Vice President Dobbs. *Of course our investments are being aptly fueled on the global market because we deregulated everything from banking and environmental controls to oil drilling and mining standards. We even refused to sign the peace treaties so that our defense contractors could build new missile and other weapon systems. Believe me Mr. President we have taken care of the details. We, the elite, are in firm control.*

It all sounds very good, replied President Burns. *I am pleased at the way you have handled everything Martin. Let me share something with you that every President comes to realize. The government really does exist to serve the common good. I hear what you say about us controlling the world. That might be a good thing. Maybe the world needs a ruling class. I don't know. If it does, I don't want to be in that number. Let me tell you something that I do know.*

If Americans ever suspected that we are trying to rule them, they will hunt us down and drag our carcasses through the streets like we were a pack of vicious rabid wolves. Comfortably reclining in an overstuffed adjustable chair, President Gray Burns looked directly at Dobbs and suddenly seemed more serious than at any time Dobbs could recall. Leaning slightly forward, the President continued. *That is why we must give the people something, even while we try to rape the world. Oh, you seem shocked Martin that I have some insight into these matters,* spoke the President.

I know that the high interest rates buried in the fine print of these easy to get; initial low interest home mortgages will cause many homeowners to default. Borrowers simply will not be able make their mortgage payments when the high end rates kick in. I don't feel good knowing that millions of Americans are going to wake up and realize that the most important asset they own, their home, which shelters their children, has been pushed beyond their ability to own.

It will hurt to have their homes wrested from them, especially by paper hucksters that simply manipulate figures and drain the life blood from good and decent Americans, expounded Burns. *Yes, I'm going along with all of this deregulation that you and others in my administration propose. I simply don't like it. Another thing Dobbs, while everyone thinks that I am not interested in the environment, I know that our planet is in serious danger. Deregulation is one of the main reasons that our waterways and atmosphere are badly polluted with toxic wastes and gases.*

Taxpayer money should be used for defense, to build and maintain the country's infrastructure, to keep the environment safe and to promote economic growth. It should also be used to insure that our people are the best educated on the planet and to push the envelope of progress far ahead of our needs. Look at what we have done Martin, lectured the President. *We gave away more than a trillion dollars of taxpayer money to a small number of wealthy people.*

That was like if you added all of the robberies in the country's history, they wouldn't come close to the money we took from the American people in that move. Ok, we made some more multi-millionaires and maybe some billionaires to be part of the new world elite, whatever that means. It bothers me that those stuffed pockets got that money without lifting a finger to earn it, stated a hyped up President as he stood and walked toward the window.

To me, that feels like a crime; and we enabled it. Rich people should earn their money, not have it given to them by poor people. The country does not need a top heavy group of greedy paper pushers thinking that it's proper to garner money by passing paper from one source to another. This type does not feel inclined to put anything back into the community. They think that their wealth is just to make them "feel good". Now those who earn their money through investment, borrowing and hard work, well they will reinvest their money back into the economy. Taxpayer money given to super rich people is basically lost to the economy.

You know what's so bad about it Dobbs, asked President Burns? *We did not create one job with that money. We did not improve one road, rail line or airport. We did not pay for one weapon of defense nor one Medicare bill nor did we write one social security check. We did not pay anything on our two wars nor did we buy one prescription drug. Out of more than a trillion dollars spent, we did not help one college student with his/her education, nor did we research a single method of protecting our atmosphere,* the President declared as he turned away from the Vice-President.

I know what rich types say about trickle-down economics. That is just about the biggest crock of all. You know that businessmen only work to build businesses and employ people when they invest their own funds or borrow against their assets. My brother had it right when he was President, Burns recalled. *He said that trickle-down economics is voodoo economics.* I agree. *I believe in capitalism. I believe a man should be able to make as much money as he can. I support a global economy.*

43

I draw the line when a guy can be a multi-millionaire or billionaire with a stroke of the pen. The people who got the bulk of the tax money didn't deserve it, lamented the President. *They will never invest that money in business ventures. Fast cars, private jets, million dollar houses, lavish parties, yachts, ten thousand dollar ladies of the night and even a Rembrandt or two is where that money is going,* fumed President Burns. Warming to his message, President Gray Burns continued, *we must do something for the every-day people.*

Now old folks are having trouble paying for their medicines. I want to give them some relief from high prescription drug prices. American pharmaceutical companies are complaining about seniors getting drugs from Canada. They even rant about old timers dying because they can't pay the high prices charged by American drug companies. USA drug companies claim they are losing customers every time some old geezer croaks because he can't pay for his drugs. So, by paying for the old timers' prescription drugs, we kill two birds with one shot.

We bring the Canada buyers back to American drug companies; and we make old folks happy. Burns, now pacing back and forth was in high thinking mode. The drug companies will make so much money from our prescription drug payments for seniors, some of these drug multi-million dollar hotshots will get to be billionaires. We will have pharmaceutical billionaires as part of our base. Most seniors did not vote for me in the last election. Paying for their drugs will bring a large number of them into my fold.

President Burns further instructed his Vice President, We *won't even have to campaign for the seniors votes Martin. We can just count on them to vote for me. I can* already *hear those democrats screaming that we have not made provisions to pay for the drug plan. We can just ignore them. I agree with you Martin. We have two wars going. I am the war President and I don't have time to think about paying for anything. I mean, hell, we own the printing presses. We can just print some more money to cover those expenses.*

I don't understand deficits and national debt anyway. I wouldn't know the difference between the GNP and the GDP. You handle the finances and congress Martin. I'll handle the wars, and Jack (Jack Rankin, Burn's Press Secretary) *can handle the press.* Burns, laughing while obviously in a chipper mood, informed Dobbs. *Anyway, I'll say it again Martin, I have to look out for the little people. I admit that I don't know why, yet I feel compelled to follow the rule of Presidents; which is if you do something big for the rich you had better do something for the poor and middle class.*

The last President explained it to me. I just didn't understand it all. I did get enough to know that If reporters, whether liberal or conservative, get to reporting that big chunks of government money is going to multi-millionaires, I better be damn sure that I did something for the average guy. I don't want the great unwashed blaming me for their misery. I don't want them claiming that I gave the fruits of their hard earned labor to a few very rich people while neglecting their needs.

Sharing some of the wealth with Joe America, albeit a puny amount percentage wise, keeps the average citizen satisfied. I mean, I don't know why you are so hell bent on making a ruling class of billionaires Martin. I think you're just asking for trouble down the line. We could have just as easily given the big shots a few million each and have them in our pocket. I don't see where making millionaires into multi-millionaires and multi-millionaires into billionaires benefit us or the country, concluded President Burns.

That's just the point; spoke Martin Dobbs, the Vice President. *We must have a society that is so rich and powerful no one will be able to come against us. Dictators are so greedy, they horde all the riches of their little shit holes for themselves. They give peanuts to their few cronies. So when the people rise up against them, they don't have any real powerful allies to fall back on. By having multi-millionaires and billionaires in a lot of different areas, we can defend ourselves on every front against any foe.*

We can take an obvious fact and make people believe otherwise. We have people in congress, in retail, in the military industrial complex, in housing, in the media, in shipping, in manufacturing, in pharmaceuticals, in transportation, in banking, in insurance, and in law claimed an obviously gleeful Dobbs. *So no matter how they come against us, we can marshal the resources to convince the masses that we are the best thing for them since coffee.*

In fact, we can also get the perennial have-nots to support most any position we take. I read on a website named medensan.com that Blacks are the only people in the country who don't have a heritage or a name. I found it so interesting, I intend to go back and read some more.

If we throw them any small bone, Blacks will support whatever we want them to be for. Because of the civil rights movement, Blacks built up a powerful activist network. Old John Fletcher, you know, the CEO of that big old soap company, told his advertising people that Blacks sell his products to Whites better than anyone else.

48

John thinks that Blacks' shrill music mesmerizes Whites; and their athleticism fascinates Whites and others. To John, Blacks are the most influential advertising group on the planet. Recently, old John said that he only wanted to see Black actors advertising his stuff. He said that if he saw too many Whites hawking his products on TV, he would fire his advertising people. When we need the Blacks, we can give the NAACP and their other groups some money. Then we get one of those old civil rights relics to say that we are right. Now, all of the Blacks will fall in line, finished Dobbs.

Burns, his interest piqued, asked, *why do Blacks vote democratic? Our party looks like a saucer of fish belly whites during the convention. I did a little study on why we are so white. Up until Kanndi made his "there is no difference between Blacks and Whites speech,", the Republican Party was nearly all black. Southern, bigoted Whites got so mad at Kanndi, they bolted the Democratic Party and took the Republican party from the Blacks,* said President Burns, ending the meeting.

Mr. President

2009

Streets on the Potomac

Chapter 4

Mr. President, it is the winter of 2009. *I am a street voice crying in the wilderness of urban America. Here's where it's at* **Mr. President Barry Owens**. *Look at street after street. Since you live in that white ivory tower and don't get to the streets, let me break it down for you. What you're going to see on my streets is nothing worthwhile. The first thing that you will notice is: the streets are literally crumbling. There are pot holes in every street and trash everywhere. The next things that you are going to see are many men. Bunches of dudes are hustling on practically every street corner, wailed urban crying voice, lamenting the street conditions. Along most every major street you will see, get this: check cashing places; many check cashing places.*

Are you asking what checks do they cash? They cash personal checks for anybody with a pay check stub and identification. Most of the checks that they cashed in the past were old people's social security checks and welfare recipients' checks. But, since the government got hip and put those payments on visa cards, they don't cash those checks anymore.

51

Liquor stores, convenience stores, gas stations owned by foreigners, car title loan businesses and dollar stores enjoy great prominence in our neighborhoods. Extreme blight sits in a highly visible easy chair on our streets. Run-down houses and commercial buildings lie in ruin, existing only to give shelter to rats, drunks and drug addicts, bemoaned urban street voice. *See the public schools Mr. President? Guess what? Very little teaching goes on in them.*

In our public school system, administrators and teachers get paid. Suppliers and contractors vie for lucrative contracts. Everybody concerned come to the educational table of plenty and get served, including the students. Except the students get the shaft while everyone else gets the goodies. Cops, drug pushers, gangs and guns are well represented on these streets Mr. President..

See that fast car with the blue lights? Oh, we have plenty of them. Where is he going and what's he doing? Why he's pulling over a run down car. See, he's giving the poor slob a ticket.

Traffic fines paid by the poor are a large part of the City's revenue. Did I fail to mention that a clerk in the traffic court's office told me that over a million dollars in tickets were collected for one day last July 4th, and ninety five percent of that money was paid by poor City residents? Swiftly striding through the City streets, Urban Street Voice continued to deliver expert accounts of urban life to President Barry Owens.

*See that new jail? It's the pride and joy of certain segments of the City. Actually, they want to build another multi-million dollar jail. Who are **they** you ask? **They** are the judges, lawyers, policemen, district attorneys, jailers, prison guards and bail bondsmen that make a living off the poor wretches in the City. Heck you already know that the judicial system is one of the biggest businesses in most every City. Add in the cheap convict labor sentenced to private prisons, and you have a huge industry that leeches on the backs of the poor and hapless. The most important link in this urban tragedy is the Black man who dropped out of school*

53

He's the one who commits the petty crime. Other than traffic tickets' revenue, gouged mostly from poor City residents, the judicial system thrives on that dude. Hopeless and Hapless predominately Black and Hispanic men are the raw materials that supply the system with the same thing every industry needs, a good product. Moreover, the district attorney's motto is plea bargain, plea bargain Keep-them rolling in, rolling out, rolling in again, out again and back in. The judges are happy, the police are ecstatic, the lawyers are delighted and the prison owners are rich. Evil in action? You bet, angrily ranted street voice.

You want to know why they don't break the cycle? Really! Then get off your only serving Washington big shot asses that you think will reelect you and come to the City streets. Ok. So you're here. Thank you sir.

Where are they? Did you ask where are the jobs Mr. President? You don't see any do you? Why is that? Well, let's see, said the urban crying voice, as he lapsed into the vernacular of the street.

When school integration loomed on the horizon; White folks took their children, their bed and board and scurried to the suburbs. Incidentally, they also took every job with them. It was like they went around with a job vacuum cleaner and vacuumed up every job they could find. They left only the nastiest understaffed poor quality service and merchandise imaginable for those left in the City. Ok, they also provided minimum government subsistence allowances to unwed mothers. The only problem was the mothers had to kick the fathers of their children out of the house in order to receive the bare pittances, stormed Urban Voice.

With no job or prospect of one, no ability to borrow to start businesses, no place to stay, and forced into exile from their families, what do you think the men did to simply survive? You're right Mr. President! They turned to petty crime! How did society benefit from this American human tragedy? Why, Mr. President, We got happy judges, ecstatic brutal policemen, delighted lawyers, grinning district attorneys and rich prison owners.

Each of these grand professions depends on that marvelous tactic of modern urban life; plea bargain. Introduce gangs into the mix and supply them with drugs to sell to the City dwellers. Add guns, alcohol and the scourge; cocaine, and you have a toxic mix of our present day life. Almost breathless, Urban Street Voice sat briefly on a curb before continuing his journey with President Barry Owens. *Sir, I'm sure that you want to know who lives in those big houses downtown and who drives those big shiny new cars crowding into the City?*

Come on Mr. President! How can you be so smart about everything, but be so dumb about the lives of inner City Black and Hispanic people. In those downtown residences are the White folks who left the City to escape Black and Latino people. They live in very secure sheltered communities located near the seat of power, which is down town. They manage the prison camps that the Cities have become. The big cars are owned by out of town workers who come back into the City every day to collect a paycheck from the poor City residents.

56

The ones in the big houses downtown are beneficiaries of urban renewal money. You know; money that came from the Federal government to the Cities for the purpose of improving the structures of the Cities for the benefit of City dwellers. What it really did was to build shiny commercial enterprises and big homes in secure neighborhoods where the returning White workers could work and live. Urban renewal displaced urban Black families, which furthered the tearing of a rip in the fabric of Black family life.

What can you do about the situation, Mr. President? Listen here sir! The main thing that you can do is invest in the Cities. The government must invest in industries that produce jobs. Get yourself a copy of that little handbook titled: [1]"The Inner City Progress Initiative." You'll find everything that you need to save the Cities in it. Now dribble that between your legs and slam dunk our Cities to prosperity, cried Urban Voice, as he disappeared in the City's murkiness.[1]

57

Mr. President, Mr. President

2010

Middle Class on the Potomac

Chapter 5

58

Mr. President, Mr. President it is the Summer of 2010. *I am a middle income voice crying from the lawn of my foreclosed home. Where is my good secure job? Where is my guaranteed pension fund? Where is the health care for me and my family? Where is my child's education? Where is my new car? Mr. President where is my home for me and my family. I feel naked and violated. This stuff was my birth right. I feel entitled to it. I thought that I was on top of the world. But look at me now!*

I don't have anything! I have lost everything! I don't even have a piss stool to sit on, moaned Middle Income Voice. *Look, four years ago I was content sitting at my desk doing my hi-tech job. Hell, I could write some of the best computer programs in the industry. Mind you, they were just add-ons to existing programs, but they made the company a lot of money. Then one Monday morning, I believe it was in October, 06, my team leader announced at a meeting that some foreigners were coming in and we had to train them to do our jobs.*

59

My co-workers and I were stunned. We thought we were being replaced. However, before we could slip into panic mode, management assured us that training foreigners to do our jobs did not represent a threat to our job security. They told us that these people were to serve foreign markets as adjuncts to our company. Training them will make our jobs even more secure was the bull that they fed us, lamented Middle Income Voice. *Alright, I put my fears aside and went along with the program. I even fell for that bullshit they sold me about the tax cut. You know; the tax give-away that swelled the pockets of the rich beyond imagination.*

All that crap about them rich folks creating jobs from that money; and the jobs trickling down to us, the middle class, was just a bunch of hot hooey, related Middle Income Voice. *Ok! So I greedily took the measly six hundred dollars they gave me and thought no more about it. Oh, I admit that I got caught up in the hype about the big bad dude in the middle east who had nuclear weapons and was about to use them on us?*

Whoa! Did you see and hear what the Secretary of State had to say at the UN? I thought the bombs would start dropping any second. How convincing was the President when he said the dude had received some pipes or other such garbage from an African country? I heard him when he said that was the final piece the Arab dude needed in order to blow all of us to hell and back. I was so scared; I nearly trashed my pants.

I was riled up and ready to kick some Arab ass because of 911. Even so, I felt a little uneasy about us militarily taking out the government in far-away Afghanistan. I wondered why we didn't go after Al-Qaeda rather than trying to control the whole country. I certainly could not see any benefit to me or our country in occupying another nation. Agitated, Middle Income *Voice went on. Hell, I knew from my studies about colonialism that it wouldn't work. How dumb do you have to be to know that every colonialist was sent packing and sometimes violently. Yeah, I began to hear rumors about the Collins surplus being gone.*

Water cooler talk about the global economy and the government giving corporations tax breaks to help them relocate American jobs to foreign countries shot right past me. Nothing bad was happening to me personally, so I had no reason to worry. As if trying to grasp the meaning of what he had just said, Middle Income Voice paused to collect his thoughts, and proceeded on. *I did have an unsettling feeling about the country that lasted for weeks. We had converted a huge surplus into a massive deficit; and nobody mentioned how we would pay for all this new stuff.*

I didn't think these events would affect me. I had my job; and I was making the big bucks. I saw Burns on TV mouthing off about how he had ordered the bombing of the big dude's oil rich country. I was like go, you know; all patriotic. According to cable news, which I depended on for most of my current events, a great majority of the senators and congressmen had agreed with the invasion thing. Cable news networks reported that polls showed that most Americans felt like me.

I was surprised but supportive. Then, like a bolt out of hell, in the midst of all the crap that was going on nationally, my work team leader informed me and my co-workers that the company was closing its doors and we were out of jobs! I could not believe what I had heard. I mean, hey, I worked my tail off to get a degree in computer technology. I had invested seven years in that company and was finally making good money. When I told my wife the news, she cried for a whole hour. Soon after, she said that she could not bear the pain of her husband being out of work, and left me.

Hanging his head, Middle Income Voice said. *What I'm talking about here, Mr. President, is my whole world. I mean everything, including my marriage, was destroyed. Man did that hurt. I want you to feel my pain Mr. President. Look, I didn't vote for the democrats in the last election because I was so pissed. I thought that if I voted for some republicans, things would get better. You already know they didn't get better; they got worse. Deep down inside I guess I knew they would.*

. I read and watch the news. I know a lot about what's going on. The way I see it is this small band of radical republicans called the **"New Party***," are going to put you, me and the country through hell during the next two years. You, because they think you are trying to change the country from a society that is controlled by the rich, back to one where every citizen has a voice,* intoned Middle Income Voice. *As for me, neither the New Partiers nor the Republicans give a damn.*

They do try to couch some issues in thinly veiled racist tones to rouse what they perceive as racism in me, simply because I am White. They fail miserably in that respect. I and most Whites in my generation were raised enjoying hip hop, rap and Black people. Now pacing back and forth in front of Owens, Middle Income Voice, almost in a rant, shouted, *we don't give a pigment's ass about race. We want some political leaders who work for us, the people, and not for corporations, the super rich and foreign governments. Personally Mr. President, I just want a job badly.*

Mr. President, Mr. President,

Mr. President Owens

2012

Billionaires on the Potomac

Chapter 6

Thank you for taking the time to hear me out Mr. President. If congress works with you, I truly believe that you can lead us to greatness. Anyway, good luck. You now have my full and devoted support, finished Middle Income Voice.

Mr. President, Mr. President, Mr. President; *it is the winter of 2012. I am a billionaire voice crying from the quiet sanctity of my inner musings. I am crying because of a gnawing fear that is deeply rooted in my gut. Just so you know sir, I am an old fashioned billionaire. My fortune came from my personal investments, bank loans, and investments by others. I have experienced both severe business losses and exhilarating rebounds.*

Whether failing or succeeding, hard work has always been at the center of my business endeavors, said Billionaire Voice. My colleagues and I have a lot to say to you Mr. President. So I beg your patient indulgence. Yes I have a corporate jet dedicated to my personal use. I have several cars that cost more than one hundred thousand dollars each. One cost more than a million dollars.

66

Enough about me. The constitution charges the Federal government to serve the common good. That means: whatever we all share in common, regardless of wealth, race, gender, religion, etc., the government must attend to it. Well here are my concerns. My personal and business jets must have good safe runways on which to land, Billionaire Voice quietly proclaimed. *Most of my work requires me to take off and land at public airports.*

Although the runways appear to be safely maintained now, what happens if the <u>New Party</u> forces you to cut spending for airports? Will we see potholes in the runways? I am affected as much or more than the average air traveler. How does my money give me an advantage there? I also fear a cutback in air traffic controllers. If I can't get high quality flight directions from air traffic controllers because their numbers have been cut, my takeoffs and landings will be delayed. I will be as inconvenienced and endangered as any other airline passenger or small plane pilot.

My money will not help me keep a timely schedule. Driving my Bentley, Rolls or chauffeured limousine over streets filled with potholes is uncomfortable and very nerve wracking. Pausing to let his concerns sink in, Billionaire Voice *continued, No matter how much money I have, I cannot fix public streets or airport runways. That is the responsibility of government. Again, I ask, how is my money helping me with these matters? Look, right now I am considering driving a jalopy rather than risk blowing a tire out, or breaking an axle on one of my high end automobiles.*

What I am saying Mr. President Owens is that spending cuts must be balanced against revenue in order to serve the common good. Maintaining our transportation infrastructure serves the common good, and must be done by our Federal and State governments. Funding must be in full force and not cut for transportation infrastructure, said Billionaire Voice as he raised his feet and placed them on the ottoman in front of him. He leaned back, cleared his throat and Kept going.

No matter our wealth or societal status, we all breathe the same air and we all are subject to natural disasters. It is very much in the common good for the government to be involved in protecting our environment. Funding for a safe environment must be increased by congress, not cut. We realize that congressmen must concentrate on servicing the needs of their back home constituents.

You sir, must always be mindful that you are the single individual that is charged to look after the needs of every American. Within that context, most Americans are looking to you for help with their divergent problems. We both hear the hue and cry from the republicans to cut Federal spending, said Billionaire Voice, while stifling a cough. *The New Party within the republican ranks is determined to cut out entitlements, particularly social security, Medicare, Aid to Dependent Families, Medicaid, prescription drug coverage, Pell grants, and early childhood development programs. Millions of good people depend on these programs. If these cuts are successful, millions will die.*

There are other cuts, but these are the <u>New Party's</u> first targets. New partiers and some republicans are using the most insidious scare tactics in their campaign to slice entitlement programs. They predict that the economy will collapse and our children will be left to shoulder the burden of our reckless spending. They lie. Each of these programs is of utmost importance to the recipients of this assistance. As a life long republican with brightly hued conservative stripes, I am somewhat perplexed by the aggressiveness of the <u>New Party</u> in going after these programs.

Their insistence that rich people like me be exempt from one of the largest tax increases in history (already enacted spending cuts) astounds me, proclaimed Billionaire Voice. Standing and facing President Barry Owens, Billionaire Voice continued, *Frankly, that type of attitude really frightens me. We, rich people who actually worked for our money, don't believe that the poor and middle class will stand by and watch, while congress rapes them on our (the rich) behalf.*

The spending cuts, <u>which in reality, is a tax on the poor and elderly,</u> do not impact us, the rich. Those of us with money got so fat off the burn's tax cuts; we can afford to do nothing. Billionaire Voice then said, *Mr. President, I told you that I would like for Dan Freeman, another billionaire, to join us. He wishes to offer some solutions to our financial quandary. Of course,* responded President Owens.

Mr. President, it is truly a pleasure and honor to meet you, Dan opened up while extending his hand to the President. Accepting freeman's hand, the President greeted Dan Freeman in a most gracious and personable manner, *the pleasure and honor are all mine Dan,* insisted Owens. *I'll get right to the point Mr. President,* related Freeman. *Our country is on a dangerous course. This <u>New Party</u> that is trying to dismantle social security, Medicare and other social programs, are so far off base that their policies, if adopted, would topple this country. You know; I'll wager that the New Party's rank and file don't know that they are being used to further corporate interests.*

71

A grave mistake was made when taxpayer money was given to the rich in the Burn's tax cut. A second destructive mistake was made when the Burn's administration deregulated everything. A third mistake was to allow major companies to relocate abroad and give them taxpayer money to help facilitate their move. Allowing these companies to bring their cheap goods back into the country without penalty destroys American jobs. Worse than that, this process is a direct attack on the middle class. Offered an invitation by President Owens to sit, Dan Freeman, a strapping fifty six year old man, accepted and sat.

Let me expand on what I'm saying Sir, continued Freeman. *Studies show that practically every great nation failed because it got top heavy with rich elitists. That is what is happening with our beloved country. The trillion dollars that Burns gave to the richest five percent was pocketed as personal gifts. That money did not create any jobs or help any part of the economy. It was and yet is used to support unbelievably lavish lifestyles.*

You inherited an **_unpaid for one trillion, three hndred billion dollars tax_** *cut; an* **_unpaid for eight hundred billion dollars bank bailout,_** *an* **_unpaid for prescription drug program_** *and* **_two unpaid for wars_**. *Add millions of home loans being foreclosed, an economy that was losing nearly eight hundred thousand jobs each month, and a global recession. You then, had the potential for the worst economic disaster in the history of the country.* Eager to get on with what he had to say, Freeman crossed his legs and continued to talk.

I certainly admire the job that you have done Mr. President. In the face of the most vitriolic abuse and down right disrespect, you have held this country together almost by the strength of your intelligence and will. You have not taken the haters' bait, nor have you responded negatively to any of them. Let's examine the problem and look at the financial dynamics that are at work now for the first time. Historically, riches were earned through hard work and the principles of old fashioned capitalism. This required that a sizable healthy base be in place.

Billionaire examples of persons who acquired wealth the old fashioned capitalist way are the computer man, the hotel and casino man, and the talk show lady. Comfortably settling into his delivery, Freeman went on. *Thousands of examples of multi-millionaire successes that were achieved the old fashioned capitalist way can be cited. Growing businesses from the bottom up is time honored good capitalism. Good capitalism creates jobs and contributes to economic growth. When the principles of good capitalism are employed, wealth is directly gained from profits that are derived from investments, loans, employee efforts, new ideas, and hard work,* uttered Dan Freeman.

Air, water and food are the prime elements needed to survive. Running close seconds to the prime survival elements are the secondary survival elements; which are shelter, health care, jobs, transportation, education, and energy. In order for society to function properly, government must have a direct role in the disbursement of the primary and secondary survival elements.

74

What is happening now is so dire for the country that I fear for its stability. With no effort on behalf of the recipients, the country's treasure is being deposited into the personal accounts of very rich people. This means that the funds required to pay for the education of a potential discoverer of a cure for cancer has been given to a very rich person by our government. The same is true for the inventor of new energy sources or locomotion methods that could make space travel affordable.

Those potentials, along with job creation, health care and infrastructure, all suffer from a lack of funds. Money needed for these efforts is reposing in the personal caches of Burn's tax cut recipients.

Of course Mr. President, we all know that the solution to giving taxpayer money to rich people is to let the Burn's tax cuts expire. I truly hope that you are up to the task this time, pleaded Dan Freeman. *Other odious practices that threaten the financial stability of the country sprang up as a result of deregulation. Regulation is vehemently opposed by the **New Party.***

*It's obvious that the **New Party** has control of the Republican Party. You best believe that congress will have strong opposition from both Republicans and New Partiers when it attempts to impose new regulations. Nevertheless, new regulations must be enacted,* opined Dan. *With no regulations, paper pushers were allowed to bury toxic variable interest rates in mortgage paperwork. These types of mortgages made billions for the banks and their paper manipulators.* Dan was intensely into his recitation as he said *stringent regulations must be imposed on all banks that do real estates loans.*

Couple the funds given to the banks through TARP (Troubled Asset Relief Program), with the money given to them from the Burn's tax cut, and you have banks that are flush with large sums of <u>unearned</u> cash. Speculators pull off unregulated deals in the oil industry by selling a barrel of oil many times over on paper. A barrel of oil that costs sixty dollars coming out of Middle East ground might cost a hundred dollars by the time it reaches an American refinery.

Industries that involve the necessities of life are prey for traders looking to skim billions off the top. Trader activity in these industries must be tightly regulated. Money that traders take from Americans rightfully belongs to the American economy.

The New Partiers keep talking about shrinking government. **Bull!** **<u>Government must expand to protect its citizens from unsavory practices.</u>** *Moreover, a strong expanded government is needed in this global economy to prevent companies from shipping US industries and jobs overseas, while receiving tax money to pay for their moves.*

The companies that do this bring the cheap goods back into the country to sell at prices US businesses cannot compete with. What is ridiculous about the whole thing is these corporations don't pay tariffs which could give the American businesses a chance to compete. I know that I am intense in this area Mr. President, said Dan who realized that he was presenting his case with excess zeal. *Not at all Dan,* answered the President. *You have my undivided attention.*

We don't need to shrink government nor should we cut any program that benefits people. Citizens must __Beware!!!__ Multi-national corporations are buying the votes of our elected officials as we speak. We need a strong vigilant government that serves the common good while keeping steady watch over its people. More paper pushing traders are acquiring millionaire, multi-millionaire and billionaire tastes. Their thirsts will only intensify!

Gaining wealth by paper manipulation, in life sustaining areas, borders on aggregated robbery. Dan, continuing to speak with passion in his voice, said, *increasing taxes on the poor, working poor and seniors by cutting programs that benefit them, and then giving those funds to the rich; will push this country into a society that resembles feudalism. The first thing that will happen is millions of seniors and poor people will die prematurely because they will not be able to pay for their food, medicines or medical care. Millions more will die from malnutrition, freezing, heat strokes and plain worry.*

The country's successful progressive financial structure, which begins with its base of the poor, working poor and seniors, will be damaged. This is already happening. The appetites of the paper pushing rich are insatiable. Unregulated trading is already making the financial structure top heavy with the rich. Phasing out of the manufacturing middle class is in full swing.

A new base will be the poor, working poor and near poor. In a haltingly curious voice, Dan asked, *don't corporate execs and members of the New Party realize or care that sending American jobs abroad and paying for the moves with our tax dollars is destroying the country's economy?*

How, you ask? Well, the goods that were once made here are now produced cheaply in a foreign country. Those goods are imported and sold in America. The money that we spend on those goods is used to pay workers in the foreign country. The wages that were once paid to American workers have been lost to our economy.

History is rife with instances where failed societies' wealth and power were concentrated in the hands of a few. Inevitably those regimes fell because the greed and misuse of power by the few oppressed the many. The people got fed up and threw the rascals out, sometimes violently. Egypt, Libya and several African countries come to mind.

Mr. President this is Mary Agnes Wallace. Mary has studied the flow of money from the perspectives of both the very rich and the very poor, said Dan Freeman as he introduced a ruddy cheeked, pleasant faced woman with short hair. Thanking Dan for the introduction, while addressing President Owens, Mary accepted an invitation to sit by easing her slender frame into an easy chair. *I am going to begin with a stark simple example Mr. President. You have two land areas that are identical in size and resources. All ingredients needed for survival and even a good life are duplicated in both land areas. Trees and vines bearing most types of fruit, berries and nuts are plentiful. The ground is fertile.*

Ponds, lakes and oceans teeming with seafood are readily accessible. Domesticated livestock roam freely. Seeds of every edible vegetable and nut abound. Neither area is accessible to the other by any means. Each area is devoid of any machinery, equipment or communication devices, such as television, telephone, radio or internet services. No contact with any outside source is allowed for a period of five years. One billion dollars is placed in each land area respectively.

One member of the New Party and his/her family are placed in one land area, which I designate as Area 1. One hundred thousand average people are located in the second land area, which I name Area 2. In area 1, the billion dollars is given to the New Party member. In area 2, ten thousand dollars is given to each person respectively. Mr. President, when revisited in five years, what would you expect to find, inquired Mary Agnes Wallace? *Don't guess I'll tell you,* continued Mary. *In area 2 you would likely see people pursuing different interests.*

81

Some would be tending orchards and selling the fruit. Others will be growing vegetables to use and sell. Raising livestock for use and sale would interest others. Learning to mill corn, thrash wheat and process sugar cane will excite some, who will then sell their services to farmers who grow corn, wheat and sugar cane. Aware that the President is showing rapt attention, Mary Agnes Wallace relaxes and settles comfortably into her dissertation. Crossing her long shapely legs, she proceeded. *Realizing that certain rules must be implemented and followed for the protection and common good of all residents and their property, money is pooled to hire a community administrator, rule enforcers, teachers and doctors, as needed.*

Funds are also pooled to obtain equipment and build facilities that serve the community, such as a school building, and equipment for a volunteer fire group. At the end of five years, you would likely see people arranged in various economic statuses or tiers. Some will operate small businesses that serve local communities.

Some will have established corporations that market and sell to the total population. Seniors and others will have paid into a retirement fund which provides income for retirees and the disabled. Some single mothers and unemployed persons require financial assistance. They get such help from the community pool. Income wise, single mothers, the unemployed and disabled are at the bottom. Going upward on the income scale are seniors and the working poor. They are followed by middle income wage earners, the well-to-do and finally by the rich. Touching her hair while adjusting herself in the chair to a more comfortable position, Mary Agnes, an attractive woman in her mid forties, persisted

Pay particular attention to the method by which community 2 attained a tier or status economy. The first act in the community after the placement of people was to award an equal amount of funds to each resident. The second act was to require each resident to contribute to a fund that was to be used for community protection and to serve the common good of the community.

83

*Many residents farmed the land. These farmers hired farm workers (working poor) to supply labor. The retirees, disabled and single mothers received direct payments from the community. They, along with farm workers, formed the **economic base** of the community. Most farmers sold their excess products to entrepreneurs who learned how to process them into foodstuffs, clothing, shelter and transportation devices. The processors sold their goods to store front merchants, who sold them to the **base,*** said Mary, pausing to catch her breath.

Other local merchants were spawned (doctors, lawyers, contractors, etc.) to service the needs of local residents. The merchants achieved a status of "well-to-do." Some national companies employed managers and paid them salaries and company stock which placed them in the rich status. Many people chose to work for businesses versus farming or idleness. These workers are employees. The businesses that hired them are employers. Some employees had to learn and apply new skills that were required by their employers.

These employees' statuses were middle income. Employees that performed work which did not require skills were part of the working poor (farm and minimum wage employees). Single mothers, the disabled and seniors received fixed subsistence allowances from the community pool of funds. The respective tier status of seniors, single mothers and disabled persons was the "poor." Each tier status occurred naturally through applications of socialism and capitalism, proclaimed a smiling Mary Agnes.

*The community pool is mostly funded by the middle class. The well-to-do and the rich also contribute to the pool. Money that goes to the non-working poor is paid from this pool of funds. The rich in this community have achieved their status through the participation of all members in the community. Simply by existing, the poor is the **base** on which other members of society build. It is the group that began monetary circulation by inputting its share of the billion dollars into numerous small businesses.* Nearing the end of her presentation, Mary warmed to her next topic.

*Contrast the conditions in "community 1" with the activities in "community 2. " In community 1, the billion dollars given to the New Party member languishes in its containers. That money is just so much worthless paper waiting to be burned or buried. There is no use for it; and there is nobody for the money to **trickle down to.** It certainly has not produced one job. In community 2, the billion dollars is currency. It creates jobs, positions and wealth as well as financial support for those who most need it. Because money flows from the bottom up, the billion dollars circulates throughout the community as currency.*

Getting to the favorite part of her presentation, Mary effused, *Ok, with no people, community 1. looks bad. So, let's put some people in community 1. Adding nine hundred, ninety nine thousand, nine hundred ninety four residents to the six in the New Party family brings the population to one hundred thousand. Acting in accordance with New Party conservative politics, the **New Partiers** in the community have formed a limited government.*

. I admit that I don't know precisely how the owner of the funds will distribute the billion dollars. However, if the new partier holds firm to the "small government" ideal, most of that money will remain in his/her possession. He/she and the few new partiers in the hundred thousand population number will refuse to give money to the elderly, even though they paid for their share. Single mothers and the disabled will likely be turned out of society to fend for themselves. Those who have an inclination to farm will do so.

*Without a base to sell to, or to invent for, a middle class will never come into existence. What you are left with is an agricultural system that is ruled over by a few **New Party** people who control the money. It basically devolves into a medieval state. That seems to be what the New Party is fighting for. Since the New Party sets the republican agenda, a medieval state appears to be what the republicans want also,* finished Mary. *Thank you for that insightful presentation Mary,* offered Owens. *It alerts us to real dangers.*

Who else do you have Dan, asked President Barry Owens? *I have James Clark here Mr. President,* responded Daniel Freeman. *Good afternoon James,* greeted the President. *I am anxious to hear what you have to say. Thank you Mr. President for allowing me to present pertinent information and projections to you,.* said a smiling James Clark, as he shook the President's hand. *Well Mr. President, speakers before me have stated that no taxpayer money should be given to the rich. I agree and I will tell you why.*

I will also talk about America's consumer base. Moreover, I will point out the bad effect which imported products that were formerly made by US workers, have on the economy. We saw what happened in the previous example when money is disbursed evenly throughout the community or is given to some rich types. The community where funds were distributed throughout thrived. The community where money was given to a few rich people lapsed into an agricultural medieval type state. No jobs were created to trickle down.

We know that money is printed based on census counts. Through government payouts and loans, money is then progressively distributed according to societal status levels. In level 1 are the disabled, unemployment recipients and single mothers (Aid to dependent families), all of whom receive minimum living allowances. The working poor (minimum wagers) and retired social security recipients make up level 2. Level 3 consists of the middle class (one hundred thousand to one million dollars). In Level 4 are the well-to-do people (one million to ninety nine million dollars). Level 5 has multi-millionaires over a hundred million and billionaires.

Gesturing as he talked, James Clark, a world renowned economist, displayed a twisted mouth when he spoke. That combined with his red hair and freckles gave this short man an impish appearance. Listening to him, one quickly got the impression that Clark was an expert in his field. Continuing, he said, *the most important people in a successful capitalist system are levels 1 and 2 residents,* stated Clark.

Level 1 residents and retirees in level 2 receive direct payments from the government. They spend all that they receive soon after getting their payments. As a result, they begin the circulation of currency in millions of locations. Without level 1 residents and retirees in level 2, most small businesses would not have anyone to sell to, and therefore would not exist, related an obviously hyped up James Clark to President Barry Owens.

Although money is printed to satisfy the population as determined by the census count, money is distributed progressively. This means that if a thousand dollars is printed for every person in the country, level 1 residents receive two hundred dollars and level 2 residents receive three hundred dollars. Higher up the scale one goes, he/she is paid progressively more. So you see Mr. President, with all the garbage that the little people (the poor) have to take from grandstanding politicians who want to cut their meager existence even more, it is the little people who prop up society through their very existence.

*By going through their everyday routines of just living, level 1 residents and level 2 retirees form the backbone of a capitalistic democracy. In other words, they are the **base** on which society sits. How you treat the poor and retirees determine whether your civilization will survive or fail. Mr. President,* expounded James Clark, now intensely into his topic. Evincing near consummate passion for his subject, it was obvious that Clark wanted President Owens to fully comprehend his message. Clark kept going, *during much of its existence, America was an agricultural nation. Farm workers were the **base** on which the nation rested.*

Realizing the importance of low paid farm workers in circulating capital, past presidents and congresses provided subsidies to farmers. With the onset of the industrial revolution, farm workers migrated to the cities in droves. The Cities did not have enough jobs to employ the new urban masses. With no jobs or other forms of income, the new urbanites turned to the Federal government for life sustaining sustenance.

All Presidents have understood the need for a **healthy stabilized base.** *Building a government sponsored base started with the New Deal under President Robertson. The New Deal produced the Social Security Act and started welfare. The Great Society, under President Jonas; brought Medicare and Medicaid into being. The Medicare Disability Act was passed under Nexson.*

Do you need something to drink, interrupted Owens? *We have soft drinks, iced tea and water,* offered the President. *Thank you sir, I'll have water,* said Clark. *I am a bit famished.* After taking a long drink from a water bottle, Clark started again. *The earned income tax credit that was enacted by Foley and expanded under Raglan; the Medicare Prescription Drug Act, under Burns, and your health care plan all signal the need for a* **large active healthy base** *that can input currency into the economy. Evidence shows that America, absent a* **healthy base** *of poor people, retirees and working poor, cannot exist as we have known it.*

In the face of virulent opposition, improvements in programs that serviced the poor, working poor and retirees continued to be made. The progressive economy produced many millionaires, some multi-millionaires and an occasional billionaire. While the country was sailing along enjoying a monetary surplus left by President Collins, sinister events were pending that would inflict deep wounds in the country's psyche and economy.

We have been going at this for several hours, said the President, again interrupting Clark's speech. *If you guys would like to take a break,* inquired Owens, *I am sure that Mrs. Bailey, she's uh the head of our culinary staff, could rustle up some sandwiches for us. I would like for Faye Logan to take over for me,* answered James Clark. *She has been charting the state of the country's economy from "911" through present and future projections. Whether we take a break or not is up to you and her sir,* concluded James Clark, finishing his presentation. *Thank you for hearing me out.*

My input into this meeting is a great honor for me Mr. President, began Faye Logan. *Forgive me,* returned Clark to the conversation, *Uh, I was remiss in not noting that Faye is a Harvard graduate. She is lauded by the Times and the Ivy League Review as one of the most knowledgeable and published experts on the economy in her field,* ended Clark. *If it's all the same to you sir, I would like to keep going. I don't think my part will be long,* Faye began again. *By all means Faye; carry on,* encouraged Owens President.

A major dynamic that the country has never seen before is at work Mr. President. That dynamic is the global economy and the manner of our participation in it. Practically every economist knows that a healthy base of poor and near poor residents, combined with a vibrant middle class, is needed for a robust economy. Our census counts the people within our borders, said Faye, a somewhat chubby woman. Brushing at her red hair, she revealed a school teacher's mannerisms, which she had been as a tenured professor in an Ivy League school's

. 94

economics research department. She was later promoted to Dean of the entire economics department. *Our progressive currency distribution and tax collection scales are tied to economic tiers. Money is printed, allocated and paid directly by the Federal government to social security recipients, disability recipients and Aid to Dependent Families' beneficiaries (through the States). Military pay, military equipment and operations, and government employees' wages are also paid directly by the Federal government. The sizes of these groups and the amounts paid to them are known.*

Because the minimum wage is set by congress, minimum wage workers' pay is also known. Certain of her facts and convinced that President Barry Owens is giving her his undivided attention, Fay Logan pressed on with her information. *The sizes of various population groups are counted by the census. Direct payments are made to residents in the low tier groups. Payouts are deposited to banks for progressive distribution to the middle class, well-to-do, rich and super rich.*

The Gross National Product (GNP) and the Gross Domestic Product (GDP) are normally projected from census population data. Here Mr. President is where the economic slope gets slippery. The GNP has historically included the dollar value of all goods and services that are produced by American companies, whether located within the US proper or abroad. The GDP has always represented the money value of all goods and services produced within American borders.

Consider what happens when an American company, A. terminates its American employees, B. relocates to a foreign country, C. substitutes its American payroll with a foreign payroll and D. imports the goods that were formerly produced in America back into the USA for sale to Americans. The President, joined by others in the room, was hanging onto Faye Logan's every word. *Now factor in that US tax money paid the company to relocate to foreign soil; and the company is charged little or no tariffs on its imports. What you have here is a perversion of USA economics, the GNP and the GDP.*

The census records the number of sales personnel hired to sell those products. Because the selling and production companies are one and the same; and it is American, the census also falsely records that the goods are made in the US. It then falsely notates that the revenue which the production jobs produce, will accrue to the American economy.

That does not happen. America only gains the wages paid to mostly minimum wage sales personnel and the taxes that they pay. The GNP and GDP are thrown curves because economic projections see American sales by a US company and falsely assigns the production costs to our GNP and GDP, lamented Logan as she remembered her surprise at the damage to the US economy these companies wrought. *This problem is acute, Mr President. Studies show that thousands of USA businesses are taking this route. While we are arguing over cutting entitlements to Americans, our real **entitlement base** is rapidly adding millions of foreign workers. If left unchecked, the **base** could expand by hundreds of millions.*

Sir, consider this reality. Money is distributed in this country by the Federal Reserve on a tier basis. From the bottom up, the major tiers are: the poor, retirees, the working poor, the middle class, the well-to-do, the rich and the ultra rich. The country's **base,** *upon which sits the middle class, the well-to-do, the rich and the ultra rich, is labeled by the census as the poor, retirees and the working poor.*

When Faye Logan announced to her two teenage girls that she was meeting with President Barry Owens, both girls squealed with excitement. Screaming with her twins; Mary and Ruth, Faye admitted to herself that she was enthralled at the prospect of meeting Owens.

An equal amount of money is printed for every resident that the census counts. Faye returning from her thoughts added, *then a progressive allocation system takes over. A dollar range is assigned for distribution to individuals that fall within a certain tier. The range assigned to the poor, retirees and working poor fall below the amount of money printed for them.*

The middle class range is the actual amount printed per person. The per person amount that is assigned to the well-to-do and up exceeds the per capita amount printed for them. Examples are a middle class worker and an aid to dependent families' recipient. If one thousand dollars is printed per resident, the aid to dependent families' recipient will likely receive two hundred dollars.

One thousand dollars is also printed per middle class worker (teacher, fire fighter, mid-level work place manager, policeman, registered nurse, etc.); and one thousand dollars is paid to the middle class worker. The upper tier individuals receive their thousand dollars plus a percentage of the residuals that accrue from the amount printed per the poor, retirees and the working poor, said Faye, as she took a swallow from her water bottle.

The President examined Fay Logan's facial expressions as she talked. It was a habit that he picked up in law school. He felt that it helped him to better grasp a speaker's message.

I hope that I have been clear so far Mr. President about what these companies that ship American jobs overseas are doing to our economy. Their activities are dangerous to our very existence as a nation. Instead of our base consisting exclusively of American residents, it is or will be expanding by hundreds of millions into other countries, related Faye as she excused herself to visit the powder room. Faye's absence signaled a break for all of the persons attending the meeting.

Returning to the meeting, Logan picked up where she left off. *Money is printed only to satisfy the requirements of people living in America. In reality, it is actually being used to pay foreign workers, their families, their retirees, their poor, their rich and their governments. Mr. President, the dollars that are pouring out of American pockets directly into foreign interests, through these companies, will make entitlements look like chump change soon. Entitlement money is spent and recycled in the US. It is counted as part of the Gross National Product and the Gross Domestic Product.*

Spending American money to buy the goods produced on foreign soil by American companies is like throwing that money into an abyss. It is akin to paying entitlements, but not getting the benefit of having that money circulate in the American economy. Can you imagine any other country permitting one of its corporations to ship its jobs here, manufacture here, import the goods back to that country, sell to their people and send the proceeds back here to pay for production costs without imposing stiff tariffs on those goods?

The United States of America teems with the natural resources of two industries; steel and hi-tech. Yet we let our corporations strip us of those industries and the jobs they created, only to watch them rebuild those industries on foreign soil. Then to rub salt in our job wounds, they flood our retail markets with goods from the relocated businesses. Faye's words were now coming in staccato fashion. Catching herself and noting that her delivery was tinged with anger, Logan paused and took a deep breath before restarting.

How could any administration condone such activity that is so harmful to America. Please excuse my attitude, Mr. President. I tend to get fired up a bit when I reflect on what's going on with this type of barracuda corporate activity. Not at all Faye, responded Owens, *I find your insight intriguing and compelling. Please continue. Thank you sir,* said Faye getting back into her dissertation. *It is demeaning to our intellect as a nation to pay certain companies to ship our industries and jobs abroad. These transfer companies should pay America for producing goods abroad and importing them back here to sell. This transfer activity is new and outside the norm. So far it has gone against our economy. Fines assessed against the transfer corporations should not affect duties placed on the goods that we sell to or receive from other nations.*

At the rate these companies are transferring our country's treasure to foreign interests; the American middle class will be severely depleted soon. You will see more mid-level managers that reflect the ethnicity of the producing countries.

Middle income workers will be forced into the ranks of the poor. The solutions are simple, explained Logan, *1. <u>Stop paying companies to relocate our jobs overseas</u>. 2. <u>Charge a foreign relocation tax to firms that do</u>. 3. <u>Levy fines and tariffs on goods that these companies import here to sell.</u> . This will help to protect American businesses that produce like goods. Mr. President, billionaire John Williams is here to continue our presentation. Your extension of the Burn's tax cuts last year put John into the billionaire's seat,* offered Faye Logan, ending her talk.

Thank you Faye, said the President, adding, *your delivery was excellent. It is likely that all of your recommendations will be adopted. Welcome John. Thank you for coming. I apologize for giving each of you short notice. I hope that finding a cure for the dire state of the economy is reason enough for you to forgive me,* laughed President Owens, extending his hand to John Williams. *We have had very informative sessions. So please proceed when you are ready John.*

Raising his six foot three inch frame from the chair in which he was sitting, and moving to stand behind that chair, John Williams accepted President Barry Owens' hand while saying, *Thank you Mr. President. I totally agree with Faye. Paying American companies to ship American jobs and capital abroad, coupled with allowing them to bring goods from those productions back into our country with impunity, is very bad for our economy. This practice is destroying our* **economic support base** *by diluting it with unaccounted for labor and the costs associated with that labor.*

As bad as that is, what's going on with our tax money and regulatory systems pose an equally grave or worse threat to the country. I am talking about deregulation and giving taxpayer money to us rich people. These two very harmful practices were implemented during the Burn's presidency. Now here I was coasting along being a multi-millionaire. Heck I didn't even know what to do with the money I had. Then out of the blue the Burn's tax cuts were passed.

Suddenly, millionaires and people who made hundreds of thousands of dollars received big tax refunds. But you have no idea how sweet the tax cuts were unless you were a multi-millionaire or a billionaire. Let's just say the tax cut increased my wealth from nearly five hundred million to about eight hundred million dollars. The strangest part is; I didn't do a thing to earn it.

You pushed me into the billionaire's club when you extended those tax cuts last year Mr. President, stated Williams while shifting position. Although he was a tall man in his late forties, John Williams was bean pole skinny. The only African-American invited to the meeting, John had quietly made his money in the publishing business that his father had started.

I'll talk first about the damaging effects that the tax cuts had and are continuing to have on the economy. The tax cuts were just a smoke screen to give rich people more than a trillion dollars of taxpayer money. As you and most economists know, tax money is never to be given to the rich.

In progressive pecuniary disbursement and tax systems, if the economy is to be healthy and vibrant, the rich must accrue wealth from the bottom up. The example of placing a New Partier in a field with a billion dollars, speaks volumes about why wealth must be earned, said Williams, sure of his facts. He enjoyed this time with the president.

Although an equal amount of money is printed for every man, woman and child living within our borders, our financial disbursement system and our tax system are progressive. That means money is distributed by the Federal Reserve based on economic status. The Federal budget contains the amount of money that the government needs for defense, its operations and entitlements.

The per capita dollars paid out by the government are stair stepped, with the poor getting the least (food stamps, subsidized housing, Medicaid, and head start). Retiree payouts are next (social security, Medicare and prescription drugs). John Williams was now getting into the meat of his presentation.

Although, he felt comfortable delivering this analysis to the President. John Williams knew that Owens was very well learned in economics. He didn't want to make a mistake that called for a presidential correction. *Federal workers, including the President, Vice President, Cabinet Officials, Senators and Representatives, are higher up the pay scale. While there are many other government expenditures, including shared payments to States for a large number of State run programs, Federal spending, as part of both the Gross National Product and the Gross Domestic Product, is a known constant*

Federal spending is published in the annual Federal Budget report. Government operations are paid with taxes collected by the Internal Revenue Service (IRS). Although the poor and retirees do not pay much in the way of income taxes, they pay taxes on every other front, including Medicare, FICA (payroll taxes), sales, gas, cigarette, property and excise taxes. His legs getting tired, John Williams retook his seat.

Like all other animals, people have two basic needs, water and food. Before farming was mechanized, much of the nation's labor consisted of many millions of farm workers. Using their land and crops as collateral, a great number of farmers financed their operations. They paid their workers' wages with bank loans. Farm workers were the country's first **economic base**

Confident that he had the attention of all present, John felt emboldened as he proceeded, *typically a large population of lowly funded residents forms the economic base of a capitalist economy. It doesn't matter whether the funds are low wages, as was the case with farm workers, or if they are small government payouts to some respective members of society (entitlements).*

The fundamental need of a capitalist society is for people who make up its **base** *to spend all of their cash capital soon after receiving those funds. This spending by the* **base***, done in millions of locations nationally, inputs and infuses currency throughout the business structure,* claimed John Williams.

Let's take a break, said President Barry Owens. *We have been at it a solid five hours. Mrs. Waters has this tray of sandwiches and beverages. Please come and partake.* Laughing, Barry Owens chimed in with; *I don't want you to think I was a bad host.* Fifteen minutes later, the meeting attendees had finished their break and returned to listen to John Williams. John and the President were both late getting back because both had calls to take. *As I was saying, before the country moved away from a farm based economy, farm workers were the dominant infusers of money into the economy*

Today, the poor and retirees make up the country's **economic base.** *They get their fixed incomes directly from the government in the form of entitlements, and input it back into the system through immediate spending,* John went on. *The importance of a* **large, low income per capita, healthy base** *to the success of a large currency system can't be overstated. Without that base to cyclic input its income into the retail system, many small businesses would not have customers.*

In other words, Mr. President, if there were no poor and retirees, there would be no working poor, no middle class, no rich and no ultra rich, stated John Williams, drinking from his water bottle. *Equally important is for the base to spend most, if not all of its money in America. US companies that move manufacturing and hi-tech jobs overseas severely damage the **base**. When they bring the goods and services produced by those ventures back to America to sell, they are destroying the **base's effectiveness**.*

Here is an example of what happens, explained Williams. *Goods that were formerly made by Americans are produced in a foreign country for $700.00. Those goods are then imported and sold here for $1000.00. The census falsely notates that both production and sales take place in the US. Based on that census data, the Federal Reserve sees $1,000.00 circulating in the US economy. In reality, however, $700.00 of that $1,000.00 was sent to a foreign country to pay production costs to workers and suppliers in that foreign country*

Mentally calculating, John recited, *this left our economy with only the $300.00 garnered from the sales money. The lost revenue ($700.00), which would have been used to purchase American merchandise, pay taxes, invest and save, is lost to our economy. It goes directly from the hard earned income of American consumers into the pockets of foreign workers and their governments. The sad part is; our financial numbers don't reflect this brutal distortion and bashing of our **base**.*

Mr. President I'm talking about the billions that go to pay the wages, benefits and taxes of foreign workers who now have the jobs that once belonged to American workers. That money, which once circulated in the US economy, does not enter it now.

With concern in his voice, John Williams stated, *the economy cannot long endure these practices. Giving large sums of American treasure to foreign interests is counter productive. Aside from being inundated with cheap goods that destruct easily, and service personnel that can't be understood, we get the financial shaft from these deals.*

Entitlements are crucial to a capitalistic non-farm economy. Aside from providing needed sustenance, including health care, for large numbers of residents, entitlements input currency into millions of economic points. They also force circulation of that currency. Unlike entitlements, sending jobs abroad drains funds from our economy, while confusing the Federal Reserve into reporting that the GNP and GDP are larger than they are..

I know I've said a mouth full Mr. President, exclaimed John, rising from his chair a second time. Settling into a standing position behind his chair, Williams spoke further. *I now come to my final remarks. It was said earlier in this meeting that taxpayer money should never be given to rich people. I fully concur with that position. Much of what has been said about US companies relocating American jobs to foreign countries can be said about giving large profitable corporations and rich people taxpayer money. Both practices hurt our economy by taking money out and not putting money back in,* proclaimed John Williams

Evidence shows that the rich viewed Burn's tax cuts as their personal bonanzas. The money was mostly used to purchase expensive personal items from a limited number of sources. In many cases, the funds languished in passive investments. Little was circulated in the economy. John Williams graduated with honors from a top rated college. He was well known in publishing circles as a fiscal conservative with a compassionate bent.

. Few of those payments were invested into any business venture. The idea that rich people create jobs, if given taxpayer money, is a myth. Reaching instant millionaire, multi-millionaire and billionaire statuses appear to be the goals of many CEOs, and traders. Giving taxpayer money to the rich is the same as sending our production dollars to foreign interests. In both cases, we are putting out and getting nothing in. Mr. President, thank you for your patient ear. I very much appreciate you taking the time to listen to me, offered John Williams, as he sat down. *You're very welcome* stated President Owens. I certainly enjoyed your talk.

Who do we have next, asked Owens? *I am next Mr. President,* spoke Richard Ferguson. Thank you for listening sir. *Others have detailed the problems. My job is to present solutions. I agree with Faye's solutions to companies taking jobs overseas.*

Her solutions are: 1. Stop paying corporations to ship our jobs overseas. 2. Charge a foreign relocation tax to firms that do. 3. Levy fines and tariffs on goods that these companies import to sell back here. Sending our industries, our jobs and associated sales dollars overseas spreads our base almost infinitely thin. We certainly can't just send that money out of the country and not have it circulate back in our monetary system.

Correspondingly, America can't continue to pour its treasure into the pockets of rich folks and corporations and not have it come back into the economy. The country needs to have all of its currency circulating in its economy. Regretfully, the nation is being badly ravaged by corporate and private interests that are causing it to hemorrhage its vital resources.

When confronted with water pipe leaks, a plumber must plug the leaks. First, however, he must shut off the flow of water by turning a valve in the pipeline to the off position. That is precisely what must be done to stop the bleeding of our currency by Americans who are immersed in greed.

Richard Ferguson had paused in his Philadelphia home to kiss his sleeping wife of twenty eight years and their three sleeping children. Richard had told them the night before that he had to catch an early train to Washington, D. C. to meet with President Barry Owens.

All the while he was getting in his car and driving to the 30th Street station, Richard's mind was racing ahead to the meeting with President Owens. An ardent supporter of Owens, he was excited to meet him. *Mr. President, please indulge me while I set the economic stage that greeted you when you took office. The economy was in free fall. American capital was pouring out unchecked at two points, which were: 1. giving US taxpayer money to rich people and large profitable corporations.*

2. American corporations were shipping our jobs, industries and revenue overseas; and US taxpayers were paying them to do so. The work place was losing eight hundred thousand jobs per month, millions of homes faced foreclosure, and the banks had been bailed out to the tune of seven hundred, fifty billion unpaid for dollars.

Add unpaid for prescription drug coverage and two unpaid for wars raging thousands of miles from home and you had a recipe for disaster that would have made the Great Depression look like a mild recession. Mr. President, It is high testimony to your steady intelligent leadership that the economy did not self destruct.

Turning a page on his new Kindle, Richard Ferguson continued, infusing stimulus money into the economy, passing your health care bill and other smaller measures prevented a head long dive into economic chaos. Those actions stopped the bleeding; and put the economy in a small growth mode. Although under attack, the nation's economic structure held fast.

The progressive (tier) dispensation and collection of funds (taxes), based on economic status, is demonstrating the toughness, resiliency and overall strength of US monetary policies. In spite of massive monetary bleeding from two areas of her economy, the country is managing to hold on. It is even showing some economic gains.

I have finally gotten to the good part Mr. President, said Ferguson. *Wonderful,* replied the President. Recalling the summary review that his staff had prepared on Ferguson, Owens was impressed with his record of turning several State economies from red to black. *Ok, I'm ready for the good part,* relayed Owens. *The first two things you must do are: stop the nation's money from being sucked from it on two fronts by greedy corporations and rich Americans. Congress must act in both causes. It won't be easy to get congressional cooperation sir. Corporate lobbyists that oppose ending practices which abuse the middle class, retirees and the poor, deeply infect capital hill.*

Lobbyists convince some members of congress to oppose everything that you are trying to do to fix the economy. Nevertheless, you must layout a detailed plan with goals that;

1. *Incorporate Faye Logan's three methods to keep corporations from shipping US industries and jobs to foreign countries.*

2. *Let the Burns tax cuts expire. Reinstate them for the middle class, but not for the rich.*

3. *Close tax loopholes on a number of fronts.*

4. *Remove the cap on payroll taxes. This will fix social security and keep it solvent in perpetuity. Every worker should pay the full twelve months of payroll taxes, regardless of income.*

5. *Strengthen Medicare by cutting out waste and fraud. Pushes for a Medicare omnibus system that combines Medicare, Medicaid and the health care plan to cover all citizens. <u>Fights the privatization of Medicare. Vouchers will kill it.</u>*

6. *Implement a plan for America's Cities as detailed in the booklet titled:* [1]*"Inner City Progress Initiative.*

7. Introduce standardized computer programs that cut out the waste and duplication in Medicare and Medicaid. When a patient's name and social security number are entered into a data system in a hospital, clinic or doctor's office, that patient's medical history will be displayed to the medical personnel that have a certifiable need to know.

Medical data that must be included are: dental, doctor, clinic and emergency room visits, diagnosis, x-rays, tests, treatments, medications, hospital stays, therapies, and surgeries. Patients must be protected from unauthorized use of their data by a password of their choosing.

8. End both wars. Keep a vigilant presence in both nations through diplomacy, intelligence and Special Forces.

9. Where American security permits, close other military bases located on foreign soil.

Pausing to clear his throat and to take a drink from a water bottle, Ferguson felt that his message was being well received by the President. He allowed himself to feel enthused and important.

Below are some suggested components of a bold new economic plan that achieves the goals that I've outlined and propels the country to the front in terms of financial stability, education and scientific achievements. Permit me to paraphrase you Mr. President, by suggesting **_invest in a national infrastructure program._** *Include roads, bridges, airports and railroads in that initiative.*

Heavily **_support green programs_** *that will wean the country off foreign oil. Green programs will go a long ways toward cleaning up the environment.* **_Construct a modern power grid_** *that will deliver reliable and cost efficient electricity to the nation.* **_Make another big push to have banks revisit home mortgage loans. Lobby banks to make small business loans, new house land loans and new house construction loans._** Lightly reminiscing, this part of Richard Ferguson's talk reminded President Barry Owens of the many times he had tried to get congress to fund these projects, only to be rebuffed.

Some small comfort crept over him as he also recalled the passage of his health care bill. The President again turned his attention to Richard Ferguson as he said, ***Re-engage the nation in a major new space program.*** Richard Ferguson continued, *according to news reports; Russia is seeking to build a space hotel within the next few years. You'll have to admit; what the Russians are proposing is exciting. While I'm not fond of space tourism, scientific space research will produce well for us as a nation. Something **like building a large space station on the moon** might be in order. Such a place could double as a hotel and as a research facility. Because of the moon's low gravity, new deep space missions would be easier to launch from there.*

Insure the good health of all Americans*. Fine tune your new health care program. Combine it with Medicare. With waste removed, Medicare is the optimum plan for everyone. Push to have all Federal health care plans incorporated into a Medicare for all health care programs.*

121

Further expounding, Richard related, *many advocates of a comprehensive solution to our economic dilemma have published articles and books on the subject. Oddly enough, there is a passage in an unusual place; a book titled:* [2] *"God's Continuing Word - A Personal Message," that I find appropriate for such a momentous undertaking. The quote speaks for itself,* enthused Ferguson.

The Clergy

8.9 Additional to concentrating on relationships between you and us, and you and each other, your plan must include the means of physically accommodating your **present and future populations.** We have told you that we are big. Our energy world is limitless and our physical domain is boundless. We need you to join us in every part of the physical and energy worlds.

8.10 Consider the small part of our physical dimension that you occupy when compared to our total physical domain. You reside on a small planet that is located in a comparatively tiny solar system. Your solar system is positioned in a modest galaxy, which travels in an average universe. Your scientists can see more than one hundred billion stars in your galaxy.

8.11 Most of these stars are larger than your sun. Although it is difficult for your scientists to view distant stars that are smaller than your sun, huge numbers.

The Clergy

of such suns exist. As with your sun, millions of objects orbit most stars, including moons, comets, asteroids and planets.

8.12 Many billions of planets revolve about extensive numbers of the suns in your galaxy. Most of these planets are larger than your planet. Vast numbers of these planets can accommodate life as you know it. These and many other types of planets can provide vital resources for your use. These resources can enhance your progress and quality of life.

8.13 Uncounted numbers of universes exist. Your scientists have not discovered one other. Your scientists have discovered nearly one hundred billion galaxies in your known universe. Most of these galaxies are larger than yours. Your scientists' tools are not sufficiently sophisticated at this time to allow them to observe more distant and smaller galaxies. Still, countless numbers of such galaxies exist.

8.14 Nearly six billion persons presently occupy your planet. If each of you inhabited one seen solar system in your galaxy, more than ninety billion such systems would remain unoccupied.

Page 78

The Clergy

8.15 Our intent is that you inhabit your whole universe. You are very fragile, very valuable and very scarce. You must treat each other as such. Your scientists will learn to travel to distant planetary systems. People will populate and reside on planets outside your solar system.

Through compassionate and fearless theology, you, the clergy must be in the forefront of that far reaching horizon.

8.16 Through invention, your planet will support your population expansion far into your future. Through compassionate utilization and distribution of invention you will prevent overcrowding on your planet. Desert reclamation, as well as lake, sea and ocean farming will

provide additional food and other life sustaining needs. Solar, sea, wind and other non-fossil sources will offer bountiful physical energy supplies. With invention, you will construct viable new communities in ocean, desert, moon and orbiting locations.

8.17 Look to other planets as new sources of vital supply and future residences. Heartily support scientific research. Encourage and aid interplanetary travel. Assure that such travel is in accordance with the mission, goals, objectives and strategies of our joint plan.

As you can see, sir, chimed in Richard, the way seems to be clear. Bold and dynamic approaches to solving the nation's problems are required. When implemented, the measures that I have recited will stabilize our financial system and dramatically increase jobs. You are fully knowledgeable of the vitriol that will greet the initiatives that I have outlined. You must use your bully pulpit to get your plan through congress.

You must talk to the American people often until your agenda is passed. Encourage the people to pressure their representatives and senators to pass your legislation. Tell them that the reasons so many qualified long term unemployed persons can't find jobs is because their jobs have been given to overseas workers. Richard, almost sermonizing, pushed on, *Do not pull punches with Americans or try to sugarcoat the facts. Let them know that as long as our country is pouring US jobs into a sea of foreign workers, or that fifty percent of the nation's wealth is being siphoned off by a few very rich people,* **<u>there *will never be jobs for them!!*</u>**

*Publicly speak to the rich. Inform them that the middle class, once bristling with manufacturing, is fast turning into a service industry. Show them how diluting the economic **base** will crush both the **base** and the middle class. Tell them that the economy will be destroyed if: 1. CEOs continue to reward themselves with huge raises and stock options. 2.. Speculators and traders keep taking fortunes by simply turning over paper. 3. US corporations continue to ship US industries and jobs overseas, while using taxpayer money to pay for their moves.*

Although he was not wealthy in the sense that he had multimillions, Richard Ferguson and his family were comfortable financially. Having studied the collapse of many dynasties, Richard had long ago concluded that the demise of most of them was due to trying to sustain the weight of too many elitists who took, but did not contribute to the economic health of their societies. *Convince the rich that if the middle class and the base are destroyed, there will be no shoulders on which they can stand. In that case, they too will fall.*

Their fall will be the farthest to travel and their misery will be the greatest. Let the citizenry know that you are fighting to end the practice of sending American jobs to foreign countries. Ask them to fight with you. Hammer and hammer again until they are convinced that their congressmen and senators will support your initiatives. Tell them to watch for a deluge of advertising directed against you and those who support your position.

Finishing his speech, Ferguson related, *big money interests will pay for this advertising. Emphasize that big money is being offered to their congressmen by corporations and other interests who want to control their votes. Mr. President, that just about wraps it up for me. It has been my real pleasure and honor to meet you. I Thank you for giving me the opportunity to make a presentation to you.* With that, Richard Ferguson turned the meeting over to President Barry Owens. *I thank each of you for coming,* began the President. *Your input will be an integral part of the legislation that my staff is drafting for presentation to congress.*

We will likely be contacting you for follow-up in the ensuing days. Again, thanks for coming, said Owens, moving out of the room and disappearing down a corridor. Later that night, while his wife and children slept, President Barry Owens reclined in his easy chair, located by a window in his master bedroom. These were times that he valued because he could think and reflect without interruption. Framed by City lights filtering through the window, the President sat; a lone solitary figure who was deep in thought and nodding off to sleep.

Do not be afraid young man. I am America's future, whispered a tall figure standing by the window. Stunned, Owens responded with, *I'm not afraid. You're the one who should be scared. Some people in this house tote really big guns.* As the President talked, he watched the figure glide across the room toward him, stopping about three feet from his chair. What impressed him most about the intruder was that it stood with its feet at least six inches off the floor. *Whoa,* yelled Owens.

I'm not some ghost that is going to take you to different places, spoke the figure, as the President was trying to determine if this intruder was male or female. *As I said, I am <u>America's future</u>. I don't want to alarm you. I just want to tell you some things that are important to your future.* Too astounded to respond, The President listened. *Tell Americans that they must vote for your agenda or be impaled on a cold hard blade of greed. Show Americans that multi-national corporations, some multi-millionaires and even some billionaires are reducing <u>America's future</u>, me, to a beggar nation.*

*They are doing this by expanding my **base** into other countries. Only the money that is paid to my residents is being returned to me as currency. My money that is being paid to hundreds of millions of workers in other countries is lost to my economy.* With great concern echoing in its voice, the figure, <u>America future,</u> continued to whisper, *the income and the ranks of my service middle class, you know, mid level managers, teachers, government workers, etc. have been sharply reduced.*

My manufacturing middle class has almost vanished because most goods are now made in foreign countries by people that earn a small fraction of my middle income workers' wages. A Republican congress and President deregulated everything a short time ago. This resulted in a slew of new paper pushers and speculators draining large sums of currency from my economy. Appearing to sigh, <u>America's future</u> whispered on.

Listen young fella, you have a great agenda that will correct the negative economic path on which America has embarked. You must vigorously rally voters to elect senators and representatives that serve the country, versus serving corporations. Absent a congress that puts the people' interest first, multi-national corporations will rule America.

*Go to the citizenry. Tell single mothers that the help she and her children get from the government will be ended unless they **vote.** Inform the middle class, working poor and the rich that the foundation on which they stand is being eroded. The country will fall under its own weight unless they **vote.***

Emphasize to retired persons that their social security benefits are already under attack. The proposal to give seniors six thousand dollars insurance vouchers and take away their Medicare was passed by congress. Insurance companies treated the three hundred billion dollars yearly voucher funds as bonus money for top executives. In your future, retirees are paying nearly twenty thousand dollars for private policies. Many seniors are dying because they can't afford health care.

Having its say, the tall figure continued to share America's future with President Owens. *Against never before seen antagonism, you are honestly trying to govern for the best interests of all Americans. Meanwhile, some CEOs of national and multi-national corporations, along with a number of super rich people, are neutralizing the* **people' vote** *by* **buying congress.** *If the country is to be saved for future generations, you, joined by the people, must fight the corporations; and win! Lobbying and donations to candidates must be tightly regulated.*

Unless stringent regulations are placed on lobbyists, it will make no difference who the voters send to congress or to their statehouses. Just as medieval societies were ruled by Kings and Queens, America will be ruled over by multi-national corporations. A good example of a society that is dominated by super rich people and multi-national corporations is depicted in the movie: "The Matrix." The only difference is that the matrix was ruled by machines, while American society is ruled by greedy, heartless corporations.

In a whisper, <u>America's future</u> expressed, *what the corporations are doing is simple. They **buy the votes** of individual members of congress. It does not matter if a campaign is contentious or hard fought, the peoples' **votes** will be worthless. The winner will be lobbied and his/her vote will be bought by corporate interests. You would think that middle income New Partiers would be most upset. Apparently these "real" Americans don't know that they are being used and taken for a ride by the "no taxes; cut spending crowd,"* said America's future.

I mean, wow! Take a look at what's happening right now Mr. President. Ultra rich Americans and multi-national corporations have attached wide open spigots to America's currency. The country's economic life blood is pouring from her economy into China, India, Russia, European nations, African countries, and Mideast potentates.

In a questioning mood, America's future asked, *why are Mexicans staying home, and others are going home? It's because American jobs have been shipped to Mexico. Mexicans are working those jobs for a mere percentage of US wages; making it impossible for American workers to compete.*

Pay attention to the members of congress who are blatantly fighting to keep the economic juice pouring out from the US economy. Those elected officials are richly rewarded by corporate lobbyists. Even if their actions hurt the country, those officials will do most anything to: 1. continue to allow US companies to ship American jobs overseas with impunity; 2. keep taxpayer money going to corporations and to the rich; and 3. keep corporations from paying taxes.

Members of the New Party work so hard to get candidates elected who actually promise to do these harmful things to the country. Regrettably, too many New Partiers are so hung up on hate; they can't see that the person destroying their way of life is the one that **they elected into office.**

Don't they realize that without regulations, a Russian, Chinese or Mideast corporation will "own" their Senator or Representative? It won't matter that a million voters braved the elements to elect a candidate who promised to represent their views. Where the interests of a corporate influence conflict with their interests, they lose. The official that they worked so hard to elect will vote the way the corporate lobbyists' money instructs him or her to vote. An example was the debt ceiling debacle.

Go figure; wondered America's future! Multi-national corporation executives have taken dead aim at the real, hard working, don't ask anybody for anything, patriotic, gun toting, "White," New Party Americans. _The question is why do the New Partiers roll over for them._

*Of all people, New Partiers should rally to your agenda Mr. President. After all, it is their middle income jobs that are most likely to be wiped out by foreign competition? Can't they see that forcing all of their elected officials to sign a pledge against new taxes is the work of corporate and foreign interests? The New Party people are obviously intelligent and patriotic. Why then don't they know that they are aiding those bent on destroying their economy? This minute, **America's base** is dying because it is forced to compete with economies where people work for a few dollars per day.* Pleased to see that his message was resonating with the President, America's Future kept going.

In my world, which is your future, America's economy has collapsed. Foreign interests own more than seventy percent of her assets. The elderly, poor and middle class have nearly disappeared. The working poor are supervised by recently arrived immigrants. Most banks are owned and run by foreigners. Elected officials are openly paid by lobbyists. Home ownership is a thing of the past.

136

*Your future reveals that Republican controlled state houses have stripped unions of their collective bargaining rights, rendering them virtually null and void. The **vote**, once a beacon that radiated the power, strength and protection of American democracy, lies mortally wounded on the daggers of corporate greed; other nations' financial attacks, and New Party hate.* Reacting as if it was sickened by the information contained in its next delivery, America's future expounded, *the bitter pill waiting in your future is that certain corporations and nations have defeated the United States of America.*

In that tenuous future, The President is little more than a figurehead. Congressional legislation is subject to approval by a committee of corporate managers. These are the legacies that congress is creating and leaving to America's children. Even now, our beloved nation is on the verge of being owned by some super rich people, multi-national corporations and the countries that control them. For those who love America, now is the time to act in the political defense of the country.

136

If America is to remain strong, both internally and externally, New Partiers and all Americans must see what's happening and embrace your policies before it's too late. Multi-national corporations want to shrink and weaken the US government so they can take it over or force it to do their bidding. The Federal government is the servant of more than three hundred million proud and brave citizens. It yet has the strength to beat back these vultures. **The country must expand and strengthen its government; not shrink and weaken it.**

Growing angry, America's future fumed. I*n today's world, the very thought of corporations being more powerful than the American government boggles the mind. In my world; America's future, that is precisely what has happened. New partiers, republicans, democrats and independents should examine today's actuality,* opined America's future. *Just as military strength is needed by the nation to defend itself from violence, so is financial and diplomatic muscle required to defend itself from virulent attacks on its economy.*

Strongly delivering its message to a President that was paying rapt attention, Tall Figure whispered in more urgent tones, w*ith the help of republicans and new partiers, corporations based in Qatar, Venezuela, India, China, Nigeria, Russia, Saudi Arabia, Brazil, Iran and other countries have fashioned a death grip on America's economy. Most troubling is that giant US companies in such diverse fields as oil, banking, insurance, pharmaceuticals, etc., are so infected with greed, that they have joined with foreign companies in placing a stranglehold on the nation.*

Americans should "get it," and join with you, Mr. President to put an end to these corporate schemes. You and your brilliant economic team have correctly diagnosed the ills that face the nation. By seeking solutions to the staggering problems that were left over from the Burns' administration, you have sacrificed some credibility and support among your liberal base and independents. It is a risk that you must take if it benefits the country.

Independents, Democrats, Republicans, New Partiers and all Americans must understand that the nation is on the verge of defeat by corporations without a single shot being fired. Realizing that it had overstayed the time allotted for this visit, America's future hoped the forces that sent it from the future would understand its delay. *Do you recall Mr. President that Ban Lidin, the leader of "El Cadia," a terrorist organization that is dedicated to the destruction of America, stated that the purpose of the "911" air attacks was to defeat America by disrupting its economy.*

He predicted that the attacks would throw the country into financial chaos; causing the nation to turn on itself. Unless America unites behind you to defeat this grab for the nation's sovereignty, Ban Lidin's prediction has already come true. In your future, Federal and State legislators are little more than corporate employees. Super rich individuals, American companies and foreign controlled multi-national corporations set and execute the nation's policy in <u>America's future</u>.

Sometimes I think that those policy decisions are made and implemented just to see American citizens suffer. Too often, enacting that policy visits pain on Americans. Suddenly, the tall figure paused and pondered. *Excuse me Mr. President. I must go and talk to the American people directly. I will return to your presence as soon as I am finished,* suggested the tall figure, while bolting through the closed window into the night.

Mr., Mrs., Miss and Ms. America, I am your future. I am calling to you from the top of the Washington Monument. Please spare me a few minutes of your busy time. I promise not to be long. Hear me! Open your eyes to the politics that are happening all around you. Your country is under attack, warned the tall figure. *The United States of America is at war, economically; and it is losing! Do you know what the sad part is,* shouted the tall figure? *America does not realize that it is fighting a deadly financial war. This is your future's urgent call to you. Democrat, Republican, Independent, and New Partier, America is calling you to economic arms.*

The US is the primary target in a world wide effort to establish a global system where only two statuses exist; <u>ruler and ruled</u>. You are needed to defend your country from the vicious financial blows that are being delivered by its economic attackers. Unless you, the citizenry, act now, the nation will lose this war. Please <u>listen and hear America</u>. Pausing, Tall Figure explained.

These are the rules of war that are designed to defeat the United States of America.

1. *Give taxpayer money to the rich.*

2. *Export American industries and jobs.*

3. *Create a one world wage structure where American wages are lowered to bring them into the range of wages paid in other countries (being forced to compete with two to ten dollars per day wages will eradicate America's middle class.)*

4. *Parcel out most governmental duties to private businesses (Medicare to insurance companies, Social Security to stockbrokers, delete assistance to single mothers).*

5. *Buy the votes of legislators in congress and in the nation's statehouses (there are more paid lobbyists in Washington than there are congress persons and congressional staffers. This year, lobbyists are pouring more money into State races than in the past ten years combined).*

6. *Kill the American dream of home ownership for most Americans. (The housing crisis has begun the process).*

7. **Oppose everything that benefits average Americans.** *Make Federal spending a scary issue that is intended to frighten citizens.*

8. *Throw mud at The President.*

9. *Shrink and weaken the Federal government to a point where it cannot protect its citizens from unscrupulous multi-national corporate practices. Do the same to State governments.*

10. *Before their eyes, and with their help, enlist and finance a vociferous group to help win the economic war against their own country; and in turn, destroy themselves.*

Peering out into the night, tall figure kept delivering his message. *See what has already been done and what is underway.*

- *Home ownership is almost a thing of the past for most Americans.*
- *The country's infrastructure is crumbling.*
- *Illegal immigrants are going home to jobs that once belonged to Americans. Unless Americans are willing to work for competitive wages, those jobs are lost forever.*
- *The country tormented itself during a debt ceiling debacle, which weakened its credit rating and ability to borrow.*
- *The government is routinely threatened with shutdowns.*
- *For the first time, America is being forced to ration disaster relief to its citizens.*
- *Unions, the bastions of middle class life, are under vicious nationwide statehouse attacks*
- *Congressman Ifa is trying to dismantle the postal service, another rock of middle class stability, in favor of UCS, Fud X, etc.*

Reflecting, Tall figure thought, *the legislators who are leading the charge against America were elected by* **New Partiers, an impassioned and patriotic section of the electorate that will suffer most from their legislators' actions.** *It is amazing that proud, patriotic, middle income people can be so blinded by hateful rhetoric; they can watch and even assist the butchers who are carving up their children' futures.*

Hear me! Oh hear me, shouted America's future. *Heed the adage: Stop; Look; Listen and Learn! Your President is besieged from all sides. He has the right answers; and he is governing for all the people. His own base is angry because they feel he has not pushed hard enough for their causes. And you, Republicans and New Partiers, know the vitriol that you have visited on him.*

I must leave this time period. Before I go, I offer solutions that will enable you to prevail in your economic war. Many commentators have convinced some of the populace that you, New Partiers, are opposed to the President because of race.

144

If that is true, why do many of you continue to vote for a chocolate Cane? Here is what you must do. Get behind your President and encourage him and the congress that you elected, to:

1. *Establish a new economic pay threshold that raises existing* **base pay.** *This action will move the income scale of America's seniors, single mothers, college students, minimum wage workers and the disabled far beyond the world's norm. Moreover, notice will be served on multi-national corporations that American wages will not be lowered to the level of other countries. These corporations must not produce their goods here for pittances and further increase their greed driven profit margins. This action will also signal that America's monetary base will continue to act in one of its traditional roles, which is to be a buffer between the wages paid to the American middle class and those paid to workers in other countries.*

2. *Enlist the Federal Reserve to raise the pay range for every status of worker. It should maintain the traditional progression of taxes and income. Applying a flat tax rate across progressive income lines would prove to be harmful to America's monetary system. It would also be patently unfair to ninety nine percent of Americans.*

3. *Identify major projects that America needs now and in the future. Prepare for tomorrow. Go bold! Go big! Declare **"newer deal'** projects that can hire millions of workers at decent middle income wages.*

4. *Although America prints its own money, it cannot supply the world with currency. With that in mind, **plug the twin spigots that are emptying American resources into other nations' and fat cats' pockets.***

5. *The **ninety nine percent** of Americans must unite now before you elect a President that is bought by corporations and will shrink and weaken the Federal Government..*

6. *The USA President is the single government official that is not lobbied by corporations. Every congressman or congresswoman has a lobbyist calling or visiting his or her offices every day. If the President is beaten down by special interests and hate mongers, the country will have lost its greatest asset. At that point, the nation will have surrendered to multi-national corporations. Every phase of American life, including the country's military and defense will be controlled by foreign corporate interests and governments.*

7. ***Regulate and regulate some more!*** *You must have a strong government to fight off the corporations. Corporations in themselves are good in a capitalistic society. They are made up of people known as shareholders. Problems exist when some large corporations funnel immense profits into the pockets of a few individuals. Neither these individuals nor their companies pay taxes. They extract*

147

money from the economy and put nothing back in. The government must regulate for the safety of its citizens. The environment, food, water, political contributions, nuclear weapons, pharmaceutical products, other weapons of mass destruction, lobbyists and airline safety are just some of the protections that were allowed to expire or were repealed during the previous administration. These and other protections must be in force if humans are to safely continue on this planet.

8. *Do not let anyone tamper with your system of government. It has proven to be the most reliable and resilient type known to man. A parliamentary form of government, where congress elects a President or Prime Minister would make the chief executive subject to congressional lobbyists that are under the control of multi-national corporations. The corporations could influence the President, who is also the military's Commander and*

Chief, through congressmen who are "bought and paid for" by the corporations. Since you, the people, actually hire the President through your vote, it is difficult for lobbyists to sink their fangs into him. No matter the political climate, the President governs for all of the people.

*Thank you for listening to me America. I, America's future, must be on my way. I implore you; do not elect a President who will weaken the Federal Government. If you do, you will have ushered in **one day of election thunder and many years of governing woe!** Do not be fearful America. Shuck fear! Go boldly into the future with progress as your beacon and success as your promise! Your way will be bright and filled with progress.*

Returning to President Barry Owens' bedroom, America's future found the President in the same chair and posture as when it left. America's future thanked him for listening and proclaimed that it must go. Then in a flash, America's future vanished into thin air.

149

Suddenly awake and completely taken aback, Barry Owens got up from his chair and walked to the window. After looking around and seeing nothing out of the ordinary, he mused, *oh well; it must have been a dream.* Nevertheless, Owens was astonished at how real the dream seemed. The President sat back down in his easy chair and contemplated the day's events. After reflecting a short while, he reached for a pad that sat on a table beside his chair. A brief interval of thought ensued. Then, President Owens scribbled a note to his speech writer. The note read; *new information to add to the State of the Union speech.* Having donned his pajamas prior to sitting, the President rose and paused beside the bed to lovingly gaze at Marilyn. *I really love her,* he thought as he climbed into bed beside her. Owens propped himself up on one elbow so that he could look at his lovely wife. As he studied her sleeping features, his mind drifted back to when he first met her.

Those were endearing thoughts that always amused him and brought a smile to his face when he reminisced. His speech to a joint session of congress lay on the table beside the bed. Marilyn always proof read and critiqued his important speeches. *I'll rehearse my speech with her a final time before I deliver it tomorrow,* mused the President. The following evening, presidential invitees and members of both houses of congress rose, clapped and cheered as the President of the United States opened with: ***my fellow Americans!***

152

Citations

---

[1] Tanner George, Retrieved from www.myicpi.com

[2] Anonymous, God's Continuing Word-A Personal Message, Retrieved fromwww.godscontinuingword.com